매 일 매 일   일 상 생 활   속 에   살 아   숨 쉬 는   영 어 !

Everyday English

Trevor B. Mitchell, Stephen L. Poirier, Baek Ju Hyun

무료 MP3파일 제공(Everyday English Listening)
https://cafe.naver.com/everydayenglish1

북넷

Preface

Making a textbook is challenging and would be impossible without the help and inspiration of good people. We would like to thank Professor Eric Gilder of the Papua New Guinea University of Technology, Professor Leona English and Professor Paul Phillips of Saint Francis Xavier University for their inspiration and encouragement in writing this book. We would also like to thank our past students who have taught us about what we needed to do in order to make this book effective and enjoyable.

Contents

Contents

Contents

UNIT 01

Introductions

Section 01 Vocabulary
Section 02 First Meetings
Section 03 Giving Better Answers
Section 04 Favorites
Section 05 Saying Goodbye
Section 06 Review

Section 01

Vocabulary

01 Practice your pronunciation of the following words and expressions.

- □ avoid: 방지하다, 피하다
- □ common: 공통의, 공동의
- □ confused: 혼란스러운
- □ conversation: 대화, 회화
- □ develop: 성장(발달)하다
- □ different: 다른, 차이가 나는
- □ distribution: 분배, 유통
- □ favorite: 좋아하는, 특히 좋아하는 것
- □ summarizing: 요약
- □ foreigner: 외국인
- □ hobby: 취미
- □ hometown: 고향
- □ interesting: 재미있는, 흥미있는
- □ introduce: 소개하다, 진행하다
- □ management: 경영, 운영, 관리
- □ misunderstanding: 오해
- □ office worker: 사무원
- □ opinion: 의견, 견해
- □ personal: 개인적인
- □ practice: 실행, 실천
- □ relationship: 관계
- □ relax: 휴식을 취하다
- □ tourism: 관광
- □ weekend: 주말
- □ comment: 논평, 언급
- □ exhausted: 기진맥진한, 진이 다 빠진
- □ completed: 완료된
- □ smoothly: 부드럽게, 순조롭게
- □ personally: 개인적으로

02 Hi or Hello?

Conversation Point!

There are informal and formal ways to greet people. Use informal ways among friends and family. Use formal ways in business situations and when first meeting someone.

Informal	Formal
Hi.	Hello.
How are you?	How do you do?
Glad to meet you.	It is a pleasure to meet you.
Nice to meet you.	It has been nice to meet you.
What's your name?	May I ask your name?
What do you do?	May I ask what you do for a living?
How's it going?	How are things with you?
What's up?	What are you doing now?

Section 02 First Meetings

01 Listen to the conversation and then practice with a partner. Practice each part.

Conversation 1 **First Meetings**

Tyler: Hi, I'm Tyler. What's your name?

Sun Hee: My name is Sun Hee. It's nice to meet you.

Tyler: It's nice to meet you, too.

Sun Hee: Where are you from Tyler?

Tyler: I'm from the U.S.

Sun Hee: What do you do?

Tyler: I'm a student. How about you?

Sun Hee: I'm a student, too. My major is management.

Tyler: My major is engineering.

타일러: 안녕하세요, 타일러입니다. 당신 이름은요?
선희: 선희예요. 만나서 반가워요
타일러: 저도 당신을 만나서 기뻐요.
선희: 어디서 왔어요?
타일러: 미국에서 왔어요.
선희: 무슨 일을 하세요?
타일러: 학생입니다. 당신은요?
선희: 나도 학생이고요, 전공은 경영학이에요.
타일러: 내 전공은 엔지니어링입니다.

02 Answering Personal Questions.

Conversation Point!

To answer personal questions like **"What is your name?"** you can say **"My name is William."** Or you can say **"It's William."** or **"I'm William."**

Examples:

Question	Answer 1	Answer 2
What is your name?	My name is Sun Hee.	I'm Sun Hee.
What is your phone number?	My number is 010 815 1004.	It's 010 815 1004.
What is your friend's name?	My friend's name is Tyler.	It's Tyler.
What is your hometown?	My hometown is Seoul.	It's Seoul.

03 Write answers for the questions and make questions for the answers.

1. What is your first name?

____

2. What is your last name?

____

3. What is your job?

____

4. What is your email address?

____

5. ____?

My phone number is 010 815 1004.

6. ____?

My major is management.

7. ____?

My hometown is Seoul.

8. ____?

My friend's name is William.

04 **Form a group of three or four people. Introduce yourself to your group members. Ask them the questions and write their answers.**

What is your ________ ?	Student 1	Student 2	Student 3
name			
major			
phone number			
email address			
hometown			

Section 03 Giving Better Answers

01 Sometimes personal questions and answers have different styles. Check the examples below.

1. How old are you?	I am 21 years old.
2. Where are you from?	I am from South Korea.
3. Are you a student?	Yes I am. / No, I'm an office worker.
4. Is Seoul your hometown?	Yes, it is.
	No, I live in Seoul but my hometown is Busan.
5. Do you have an email address?	Yes, it's niceguy@wildfire.com.
6. What do you study at your school?	I study distribution marketing.

02 How to give better answers.

Conversation Point!

Giving longer answers with more information makes your conversation sound more intelligent and interesting. Check the examples and try to make longer answers to the questions given below.

Q: Where are you from?	I am from Incheon, South Korea.
Q: Are you a student?	Yes, I study tourism management at Fraser University.
Q: Where do you live?	I live in Namdang Gu, Incheon.
Q: What is your job?	I'm an engineer. I work at Posco.
Q: Do you have a brother?	Actually, I have a brother and two sisters.

03 Answer the questions. Give as much extra information as you can.

1. Where are you from? ______________________________
2. Are you a student? ______________________________
3. Where is your hometown? ______________________________
4. What does your best friend do? ______________________________
5. What kind of sports do you like? ______________________________
6. Where do you live now? ______________________________
7. How do you come to school every day? ______________________________
8. How many people are in your family? ______________________________

Tip

When you go to another country and foreigners ask you where you are from, be sure to tell them you are from South Korea. If you say you are from Korea foreigners might be confused and ask if you are from North Korea. Foreign people have a different opinion of North Korea so you should be clear and tell them you are from South Korea to avoid any misunderstanding.

04 Form groups of three students. Ask your group members the questions and write their answers.

	Student 1	Student 2	Student 3
Where do you live?			
What are your plans this weekend?			
What kind of job do you want?			
Do you have a sister?			
Do you have a hobby?			

Section 04 Favorites

Conversation Point!

Talking about favorites is a great way to learn about other people and continue a conversation after you have introduced yourself. Learning about common interests is a great way to develop a friendly relationship.

01 Listen to the conversation and then practice it with your partner.

Conversation 2 **Favorites**

June: Are you enjoying your stay here in Korea?

Sally: Yes, I am. I really like Korean food.

June: What is your favorite Korean food?

Sally: My favorite Korean food is bulgogi.

June: I know a great bulgogi restaurant nearby. Would you like to join me for lunch?

Sally: Sure, I'd love to.

준: 한국에서의 체류가 즐거운가요?
샐리: 예. 한국음식을 매우 좋아해요.
준: 당신이 가장 좋아하는 한국음식은 무엇인가요?
샐리: 내가 가장 좋아하는 음식은 불고기예요.
준: 바로 가까이에 멋진 불고기 레스토랑을 알고 있어요. 나와 함께 점심 같이 할까요?
샐리: 좋아요. 그러고 싶어요.

02 Answer the following questions and then practice them together with your partner.

1. What is your favorite food? ______________________________.
2. What is your favorite sport? ______________________________.
3. What is your favorite kind of juice? ______________________________.
4. What is your favorite website? ______________________________.
5. What is your favorite class? ______________________________.
6. What is your favorite kind of movie? ______________________________.
7. What is your favorite book? ______________________________.
8. What is your favorite kind of coffee? ______________________________.
9. What is your favorite kind of pizza? ______________________________.
10. What is your favorite computer game? ______________________________.
11. Who is your favorite movie star? ______________________________.
12. What is your favorite TV program? ______________________________.
13. What is your favorite kind of music? ______________________________.
14. What is your favorite way to relax? ______________________________.

03 Try to make questions about favorites that fit the answers.

1. ______________________________? Fifa Online is my favorite game.
2. ______________________________? The cappuccino here is the best.
3. ______________________________? Let's get the pepperoni pizza.
4. ______________________________? I really like hip hop music.
5. ______________________________? I think Brad Pitt is a very good actor.
6. ______________________________? I love watching baseball.

Section 05 Saying Goodbye

01 Listen to the conversation and then practice it with your partner. Take turns doing each part.

Conversation 3 **Saying Goodbye**

Brian: Thank you for showing me that new movie theater.

Na Ra: No problem, Brian. I know you like movies and this place was nearby.

Brian: Maybe next week we can come here again with some of our classmates from school.

Na Ra: That's a great idea. Well, I have to meet my brother soon. I'll see you in class next week.

Brian: Have a good day, Na Ra.

Na Ra: You too, bye.

브라이언: 새 영화관을 알려 주어서 감사해요.
나라: 별말씀을요, 브라이언. 당신이 영화를 좋아하는 것을 알고 있고 이곳은 가깝게 있었어요.
브라이언: 아마 다음주나 학교 급우들 중 몇 명과 함께 이곳에 다시 올 수도 있어요.
나라: 좋은 생각이군요. 그런데, 곧 나의 동생을 만나야 해요. 다음주 수업시간에 만나요.
브라이언: 좋은 하루되세요, 나라.
나라: 당신도, 안녕.

02 Ways to Say Goodbye.

- Goodbye.
- Bye-bye.
- See you later.
- See you next time.
- Have a nice day.
- Have a good night.
- Take care.
- It's been good talking with you.
- It was a pleasure to meet you.
- It was nice to see you.

Tip

When saying goodbye and you want to add a final comment before you leave, you can add a sentence summarizing your experience.

Ex) I really had a great time. See you next class.
Ex) I had a lot of fun. Have a good night.
Ex) I hope we can do this again. Have a nice day.
Ex) I'm exhausted. Take care.

03 Write closing comments or goodbyes for each statement.

1. __________________________________. See you later.
2. __________________________________. It was a pleasure to meet you.
3. __________________________________. It was nice to see you.
4. __________________________________. Goodbye.
5. __________________________________. Bye-bye
6. We look forward to seeing you again. ______________________________
7. I'm glad this project is finally completed. ____________________________
8. I'm so happy everything went smoothly. ____________________________

>>Talking about Goodbyes.

Ask and answer the questions together with your partner.

1. Can you think of a time you were happy to say goodbye?

____

____

2. Can you think of a time you were not happy to say goodbye?

____

____

3. In your culture how is saying goodbye to old people different from young people?

____

____

4. Is how you say goodbye on the Internet different from how you say it personally?

____

____

5. What do you think of long goodbyes?

____

____

Section 06

Review

01 Match the questions with the best response.

Questions		Answers
1. What is your favorite Korean food?	____	a. I like to buy things online.
2. Where are you from?	____	b. You, too.
3. Where do you live?	____	c. I'll take green if you have it.
4. What is your name?	____	d. I like bibimbab the most.
5. What is your favorite kind of tea?	____	e. His name is Jung Hoon.
6. What is your friend's name?	____	f. I am from South Korea.
7. Have a nice day.	____	g. I live in Yongin, Kyonggi-do.
8. What is your favorite sport?	____	h. No, but I have 2 sisters.
9. Do you have a brother?	____	i. I like football the most.
10. Where is your favorite place to shop?	____	j. My name is David.

UNIT 02

Jobs

Section 01 Vocabulary

Section 02 Conversation 1

Section 03 Conversation 2

Section 04 Conversation 3

Section 01

Vocabulary

- □ assembly line: 조립라인
- □ assistant manager: 대리, 부지배인
- □ bossy: 권위적인, 으스대는
- □ candidate: 지원자, 후보자
- □ careless: 부주의한
- □ confident: 자신감있는, 확신하는
- □ current employer: 현 고용주
- □ dangerous: 위험한
- □ daycare: 데이케어[주간보호]
- □ efficient: 효율적인
- □ employee: 종업원
- □ employer: 고용주, 고용인
- □ employment history: 근무경력
- □ end date: 마감일
- □ fearless: 두려움을 모르는
- □ fit in: 어울리다
- □ flight attendant: 승무원
- □ honest: 정직한
- □ impatient: 참지못하는, 조급한
- □ interacting: 소통, 교류, 상호작용
- □ job application: 구직
- □ job duties: 직무
- □ job position: 직위
- □ minimum wage: 최저임금
- □ most recent employer: 가장 최근의 고용주
- □ nasty: 끔찍한, 형편없는
- □ negative characteristics: 부정적인 특성
- □ occupation: 직업
- □ overcome: 극복하다
- □ personal information: 개인정보
- □ positive characteristics: 긍정적인 특성
- □ procurement: 조달[입수]
- □ relationship: 관계
- □ reliable: 신뢰할 수 있는
- □ responsibility: 책임, 책무
- □ satisfaction: 만족
- □ seasonal: 계절적인
- □ sensible: 분별있는, 합리적인
- □ sensitive: 민감한, 세심한
- □ shift supervisor: 교대근무 감독자
- □ signature: 서명
- □ start date: 시작일
- □ starting pay: 초임급
- □ storefront: 가게[점표] 앞에 딸린 공간
- □ strange: 이상한, 낯선
- □ supervisor: 감독관, 관리자
- □ tough: 힘든, 어려운
- □ trustworthy: 신뢰할 수 있는
- □ unique: 유일한, 독특한
- □ witty: 재치있는

Section 02 Conversation 1

01 Listen to the following conversation and practice it with a partner.

Min Su: Hi, Jessica. Long time no see.

Jessica: Hi, Min Su. It's good to see you. Do you work around here?

Min Su: Yes, I work over there in the Samsung building. I started a new job there about 4 months ago.

Jessica: Congratulations on your new job. How do you like it?

Min Su: I like it a lot. It can be stressful at times because I have to make sure every detail is perfect. But they treat me well and it's sometimes a lot of fun.

Jessica: That is so good to hear. I work around here too, so maybe we should meet for coffee sometime.

민수: 안녕 제시카. 오랜만이군요.

제시카: 안녕 민수. 만나서 반갑군요. 이곳 근처에서 일하세요?

민수: 예, 저쪽에 있는 삼성 빌딩에서 일하고 있어요. 거기에서 4개월 전쯤 새로운 일을 시작했어요.

제시카: 새로운 직업을 갖게된 걸 축하해요. 새로운 일은 어떠세요?

민수: 무척 좋아해요. 세세한 것까지도 반드시 완벽해야 하기 때문에 때로는 스트레스가 될 수 있어요. 그렇지만 회사는 나에게 잘해주고 있고 가끔은 매우 재미있어요.

제시카: 잘 됐군요. 나역시 이 근처에 일하고 있어요. 아마 가끔 만나서 커피를 마실지도 모르겠군요.

02 Some people do not have jobs. Below are some examples of people like this:

- students
- unemployed people
- retired people
- injured workers
- housewives
- househusbands
- children

03 Answer the following questions.

1. What kind of job do you want to have someday?

____

2. What kind of job do you want to avoid?

____

3. What is the best job in Korea?

____

4. What is the worst job in Korea?

____

5. Do you want to work in Seoul?

____

04 Job Descriptions.

Match the following jobs with their descriptions.

Description		Jobs
1. protects people from criminals	____	A. fisherman
2. works at a school and instructs students	____	B. civil servant
3. makes computer programs	____	C. tailor
4. takes care of sick and injured people	____	D. teacher
5. works for the government	____	E. waitress/waiter
6. creates marketing plans	____	F. police officer
7. serves food in a restaurant	____	G. fireman
8. puts out fires	____	H. marketer
9. makes clothing	____	I. doctor
10. catches seafood	____	J. programmer

05 Job Duties.

Answer the questions about job duties.

1. What does a travel agent do? ________________________________
2. What does a chef do? ________________________________
3. What does an engineer do? ________________________________
4. What does a farmer do? ________________________________
5. What does a delivery person do? ________________________________
6. What does a flight attendant do? ________________________________
7. What does a nurse do? ________________________________
8. What does a soldier do? ________________________________
9. What does a daycare worker do? ________________________________
10. What does an assembly line worker do? ________________________________

Section 03 Conversation 2

01 Listen to the conversation and practice it with your partner.

Michael: Ashley you look so tired this morning. Are you ok?

Ashley: I'm exhausted right now. I didn't get enough sleep last night and my new job after school is really difficult.

Michael: You go to school all day and then work all evening? That must be tough. What kind of job did you get?

Ashley: I work as a waitress in a restaurant after school. I start at 6 PM when the restaurant is really busy. It doesn't close until 11 PM. I don't get home until 12:30 at night.

Michael: How many days a week do you work there?

Ashley: I work 4 days a week from Thursday to Sunday. It's when they are the busiest. I'll be ok though. It'll just take me time to get used to it.

마이클: 애쉴리, 오늘 아침 아주 피곤해 보이는군요. 괜찮아요?

애쉴리: 지금 지쳐 있어요. 지난 밤에 충분한 수면을 취하지 못해서 방과 후에 새로운 일을 하기에는 어렵겠어요.

마이클: 하루종일 학교에서 공부하고 그런 다음 저녁에 일한다고요? 고단하겠군요. 어떤 일을 구했는데요?

애쉴리: 방과 후 레스토랑에서 여종업원으로 일해요. 오후 6시에 시작하는데 레스토랑은 정말 바빠요. 오후 11시가 되어야 문을 닫아요. 밤 12시 30분이 되어서야 집에 도착해요.

마이크: 그곳에서 일주일에 며칠간 일해요?

애쉴리: 목요일부터 일요일까지 일주일에 4일 일해요. 가장 바쁜 때거든요. 그러나 괜찮을 거예요. 익숙해지는데는 시간이 걸리겠지만요.

02 Part-Time Work.

Talk about the following questions.

1. Do you have a part time job?
2. Do any of your friends have a part time job? What is it?
3. What is the minimum wage in Korea?
4. Do you think the government should raise the minimum wage?
5. How much do you think is a reasonable minimum wage?

03 Job Survey.

Try to find the perfect job by asking your partner the following questions.

1. Do you want a job where you talk to people? ______________________
2. Do you want to work from 9 AM to 5 PM? ______________________
3. Do you want a job helping people? ______________________
4. Do you want to work with a computer? ______________________
5. Do you want to perform in front of people? ______________________
6. Do you want to work at home? ______________________
7. Do you want to work outdoors? ______________________
8. Do you want a job where you travel a lot? ______________________
9. Do you want to have your own office? ______________________
10. Do you want to wear a uniform? ______________________
11. Do you want an exciting job? ______________________
12. Would you do a dangerous high paying job? ______________________
13. Would you do a stressful high paying job? ______________________

04 Complete the job application below.

Application for Employment

Date of Application: ____________________ Date Available to Start: ____________________

MY AVAILABILITY & JOB POSITION (CHECK ALL THAT APPLY)									
POSITION	STATUS	HOURS OF AVAILABILITY							
____ Storefront ____ Production ____ Shift Supervisor ____ Assistant Manager ____ Manager	____ Full-time ____ Part-time		Mon	Tue	Wed	Thurs	Fri	Sat	Sun
		From							
	Pay Expectation:	To							

MY PERSONAL INFORMATION

First Name: ______________________________ Last Name: ______________________________

Street Address: ____

City: ____

Home Phone #: ________________ Cell Phone: ________________ Email: ________________

MY EMPLOYMENT HISTORY

Current/Most Recent Employer: ______________ Can we contact this company? ____ Yes ____ No

Company: ________________ Start Date: ___________________ End Date: ________________

Supervisor: ____________________________ Phone Number: ____________________________

Position/Duties: ____

Reason for Leaving: ___________________ Starting Pay: ____________ Ending Pay: ____________

Have you ever worked at our company before? ____ Yes ____ No

If so, which location? ______________________________ Store # ____________________________

Why did you leave? _______________________________________

EDUCATION & ACTIVITIES

Please specify level of education completed: ____

What hobbies and/or activities are you involved in: ____

REFERENCES

NAME	OCCUPATION	RELATIONSHIP	PHONE NUMBER

____

Signature Date

05 Brainstorming.

Teacher and students together should make interview questions based upon the job application.

Ex) Where did you go to school?

1. ______________________________

2. ______________________________

3. ______________________________

4. ______________________________

5. ______________________________

06 Interview your Partner.

Exchange books with your partner. Check their completed job application and ask your partner some interview style questions based upon the examples above.

파트너와 책을 교환하세요. 입사지원서 작성을 완료했는지 체크하고 상기예를 근거로 하는 인터뷰스타일의 질문을 파트너에게 해보세요.

Section 04 Conversation 3

01 Listen to the conversation and practice it with your partner.

Jin Hee: We have 2 applicants to choose from. Which one should we give the job to?

Christopher: Their education and experience is similar so maybe we should look at their different characters.

Jin Hee: Candidate number 1 seems to be very smart and talented, but also rude.

Christopher: I agree. Candidate number 2's strong points are that she seems to be kind and reliable, but she is also a little bit shy.

Jin Hee: We should pick someone who will fit in well with the team. So I think candidate number 2 might be a better choice. Over time she will overcome her shyness.

Christopher: That's true and candidate number 1 may have some difficulty interacting with the other team members. Candidate number 2 is the best choice.

진희: 선택해야 할 2 사람의 지원자가 있어요. 어떤 지원자에게 일자리를 주어야 할까요?

크리스토퍼: 그들의 교육과 경력은 유사하므로 그들의 상이한 특성을 살펴보아야겠어요.

진희: 1번 지원자는 매우 똑똑하고 재능이 있어 보이지만 또한 무례해 보여요.

크리스토퍼: 그래요. 2번 지원자의 강점은 친절하고 신뢰감이 있어 보이지만 또한 다소 수줍어해요.

진희: 팀에 잘 어울리는 누군가를 뽑아야 해요. 그래서 나는 2번 지원자가 아마도 더 좋은 선택일 것으로 생각해요. 시간이 지나면 그녀는 수줍음이 없어지겠지요.

크리스토퍼: 맞아요. 1번 지원자는 다른 팀원과 상호교류의 어려움을 겪을지 모르겠어요. 2번 지원자가 최선의 선택이군요.

02 Character Traits.

Look at the character traits in the box below and list them either under positive characteristics or negative characteristics.

athletic	fearless	gentle	nasty	sensible	strange
boring	foolish	honest	outgoing	sensitive	talented
bossy	friendly	impatient	reliable	serious	trustworthy
careless	efficient	kind	rude	shy	unique
confident	generous	mean	selfish	smart	witty

Positive Characteristics	Negative Characteristics

03 More Talk about Jobs.

Make a team of three people and ask each other the following questions.

1. What jobs do you think are important? Why?
2. What jobs are very dangerous but pay well?
3. What is more important to you, money or job satisfaction?
4. How much vacation time should a person get each year?
5. When do people generally retire in your country?
6. Is there any job you would never do? What is it?
7. What skills are the most important when looking for a job?
8. What characteristics do employers look for in an employee?

UNIT

03

Family

Section 01

Vocabulary

□ army service: 군복무

□ babysit: 아이를 봐주다

□ considered: 깊이 생각한, 중시되는

□ deceased: 사망한, 고인

□ department: 부서[부처/학과]

□ discussed: 논의된

□ forgive: 용서하다

□ good manner: 바른 예의

□ misunderstand: 오해하다

□ passed away: 사망하다[돌아가시다]

□ recently: 최근에

□ relative: 비교상의, 친척

□ respectfully: 공손하게, 정중하게

□ sensitive : 세심한, 감성있는

□ throughout: 도처에, ~동안 죽, 내내

□ unemployed: 실직한(the unemployed – 실업자)

>> Words for Family and Lifestyles.

immediate family	step mother / father	fiancé / fiancée
extended family	married	single parent
adopted	partner	same sex couple
only child	divorced	
step brother / sister	single	

Try to put the family and lifestyles vocabulary in the correct blank.

1. Tyler lives with his mom but not with his dad because his parents are ______________.

2. She doesn't have any brother or sisters so she is an ______________________________.

3. He has two dads but no mom because his parents are a __________________________.

4. They are not her biological parents so she must be ______________________________.

5. I went to the wedding to see them get ____.

Section 02 Conversation 1

01 Listen to the conversation and practice it with your partner.

Brandon: Do you have a big family?

Hannah: There are four people in my family: my mother, father, my older brother, and me.

Brandon: What do they do for a living?

Hannah: My brother just finished his army service, my father is an office worker, and my mom is a housewife.

Brandon: What was your brother's job in the army?

Hannah: He drove a truck and delivered supplies.

브랜던: 대가족인가요?

한나: 내 가족에는 어머니, 아버지, 오빠, 그리고 나 네 사람이 있어요.

브랜던: 그들은 무슨 일을 하세요?

한나: 오빠는 군복무를 갓 마쳤고, 아버지는 사무원 그리고 어머니는 가정주부세요.

브랜던: 오빠는 군에서 어떤 일을 했나요?

한나: 트럭 운전과 보급품을 운반했어요.

Section 03 Family Tree

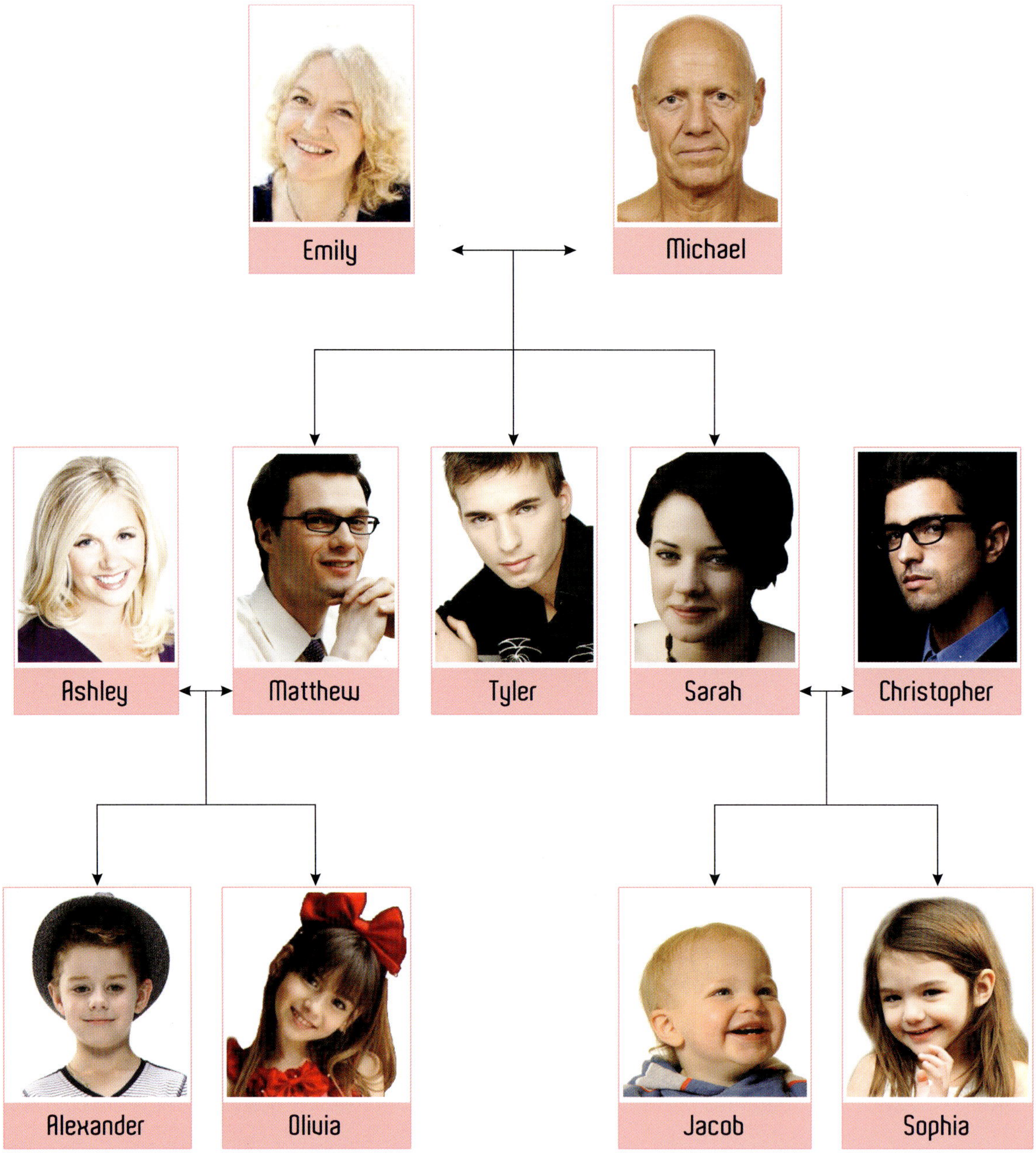

01 Family.

Immediate Family

· Matthew is Ashley's husband and Alexander and Olivia's father.

· Ashley is Matthew's wife and Alexander and Olivia's mother.

· Ashley and Matthew are Alexander and Olivia's parents.

· Alexander is Ashley and Matthew's son. Olivia is their daughter.

· Olivia is Alexander's sister. Alexander is Olivia's brother.

Extended Family

· Michael is Alexander and Olivia's grandfather. Emily is their grandmother.

· Michael and Emily are Alexander and Olivia's grandparents.

· Alexander is Michael and Emily's grandson. Olivia is their granddaughter.

· Tyler and Christopher are Alexander and Olivia's uncles.

· Sarah is Alexander and Olivia's aunt.

· Alexander is Tyler, Sarah and Christopher's nephew. Olivia is their niece.

· Jacob and Sophia are Alexander and Olivia's cousins.

· Ashley is Michael and Emily's daughter-in-law. Christopher is their son-in-law.

· Ashley is Tyler and Sarah's sister-in-law.

· Christopher is Matthew and Tyler's brother-in-law.

02 Fill in the blanks using family words.

1. Sarah is Jacob and Sophia's ______________________________.

2. Christopher is Jacob's ______________________________.

3. Jacob is Christopher's ______________________________.

4. Sarah and Christopher are Jacob and Sophia's ______________________.

5. Tyler and Matthew are Sophia's ______________________.

6. Ashley is Jacob and Sophia's ______________________.

7. Jacob is Emily and Michael's ______________________.

8. Jacob is Tyler's ______________________.

9. Sophia and Olivia are Tyler's ______________________.

10. Alexander is Sophia's ______________________.

11. Christopher is Tyler's ______________________.

12. Ashley is Sarah's ______________________.

Tip

When speaking about all of your extended family you can refer to them as your relatives. All family members including immediate family and extended family can be referred to as your family and relatives.

Ex) My family and relatives will meet at my uncle's house for Chuseok.

03 Answer the questions about your family.

1. How many people are in your family? ______________________

2. What is your father's name? ______________________

3. What is your mother's name? ______________________

4. Do you have any brothers and sisters? ______________________

5. Are your brothers and sisters older or younger than you? ______________________

6. Do you have many aunts and uncles? ______________________

7. Who is your favorite relative? ______________________

Section 04 Conversation 2 – The Past Tense

01 Listen to the following conversation and practice it with your partner.

Kayla: Where did you work before entering this company?

Ryan: I worked in the marketing department at Samsung Electronics for 5 years.

Kayla: What did you study in university?

Ryan: I studied distribution marketing. My education really fit well with my job.

Kayla: That's wonderful to hear. Did you have a hard time finding work after you graduated?

Ryan: I was unemployed for about 6 months after I finished school. But I found a job through a friend.

카일라: 이 회사에 입사하기 전 어디에서 일을 했나요?
라이언: 삼성전기 마케팅 부에서 5년간 일했어요.
카일라: 대학에서 무엇을 공부했나요?
라이언: 유통마케팅을 공부했어요. 내 직업과 아주 잘 맞아요.
카일라: 듣던 중 반가운데요. 졸업 후에 직장을 구하는 데 어려웠나요?
라이언: 졸업 후 6개월 정도 실업상태였어요. 그러나 친구를 통해 일자리를 구했어요.

02 Past Tense.

Regular verbs in the past simple tense end in **d**, **ed**, and **ied**. The pronunciation is usually a (d) sound but sometimes a (t) sound or an (id) sound.

Examples:

• work – worked	• cook – cooked	• travel – traveled
• play – played	• turn – turned	• help – helped
• jump – jumped	• paint – painted	• clean – cleaned

03 Make a sentence using the past tense forms of the following verbs.

1. work ______________________

2. marry ______________________

3. stop ______________________

4. arrive ______________________

5. study ______________________

6. graduate ______________________

7. educate ______________________

8. cheer ______________________

9. fire ______________________

10. remember ______________________

11. fail ______________________

12.complete ______________________

Irregular verbs in the past simple tense have no pattern and have various spellings. You must study these.

Examples:

• have – had	• meet – met	• take – took
• go – went	• drink – drank	• forget – forgot
• eat – ate	• see- saw	• sleep - slept

04 Make a sentence using the past tense form of these verbs.

1. pay ______________________________

2. bring ______________________________

3. drink ______________________________

4. come ______________________________

5. read ______________________________

6. babysit ______________________________

7. bind ______________________________

8. beat ______________________________

9. catch ______________________________

10. freeze ______________________________

11. forgive ______________________________

12. shut ______________________________

05 Travel Talk.

Ask your partners about their last vacation.

	Student 1	Student 2	Student 3
Where did you go?			
When did you go?			
How did you travel?			
How long did it take to get there?			
Where did you stay?			
Who did you go with?			
Where did you sleep?			
How long did you stay?			
Who did you meet?			
What did you buy?			
How much money did you spend?			
What else did you do?			

06 Past Tense Time Expressions.

Practice the following past time expressions.

• yesterday	• last Friday	• one hour ago
• the day before yesterday	• last weekend	• 2 days ago
• last night	• last summer	• a moment ago
• last week	• last winter	• a while ago
• last month	• last Chuseok	• this morning
• last year	• five minutes ago	• earlier today

>> Past Time Practice

Complete the sentences.

1. ______________________________ yesterday.

2. ______________________________ last weekend.

3. ______________________________ last summer.

4. ______________________________ five minutes ago.

5. ______________________________ two days ago.

6. ______________________________ last night.

7. ______________________________ this morning.

8. ______________________________ earlier.

Section 05 Conversation 3

01 Listen to the conversation and practice it with your partner.

Emily: When you were a child what games did you like to play?

June: I think I played everything when I was a child. I was a very active kid.

Emily: Did you play a lot of sports?

June: Yes, I did. My parents enrolled me in football, badminton, and taekwondo classes. What about you?

Emily: I mostly played computer games when I was young. But I sometimes played badminton. Maybe we should play a game sometime.

June: That's a great idea.

에밀리: 당신이 어렸을 때 무슨 게임 하기를 좋아했나요?

준: 내가 어렸을 때는 모든 것을 다해 봤어요. 나는 매우 활동적인 아이였어요.

에밀리: 당신은 많은 운동을 했나요?

준: 예. 나의 부모님은 축구, 배드민턴 그리고 태권도 반에 등록해 주셨어요. 당신은요?

에밀리: 나는 어렸을 때 주로 컴퓨터 게임을 했어요. 그러나 때때로 배드민턴을 했어요. 가끔 게임을 하는 것도 괜찮겠군요.

준: 좋은 생각이군요.

02 Using "When" to talk about the past.

Tip

The expression "when" can be used to speak about something that happened at a previous time.

Ex) When I graduated from high school, I got a part time job.
Ex) When I entered the room everyone was surprised.

Try completing the sentences below in the past tense.

1. When I entered university ______________________________.

2. When I was a high school student ______________________________.

3. When I met my friends ______________________________.

4. When I met my relatives ______________________________.

5. When I woke up this morning ______________________________.

6. When I met my new English teacher ______________________________.

7. When I last took a vacation ______________________________.

8. When I last cooked ______________________________.

9. When I ate bondeggi for the first time ______________________________.

10. When my friend drank soju ______________________________.

Section 06 Speaking About the Deceased

In most cultures throughout the world, it is considered good manners to speak respectfully when talking about the dead. This is a very sensitive topic for many people so be careful when discussing people who have passed away.

If you are asked about a family member or relative who has died your answer should use a past time expression telling the other person how long ago the person died. If you do not use a time expression, the person you are speaking with may misunderstand and think your family member has died recently and you are very sad now. If you are asked about a family member who has died you can answer the question like this.

Ex) What does your father do? — My father passed away 6 years ago.

Ex) Do you have a sister? — My sister died when she was a baby.

UNIT

04

Numbers & Money

Section 01 Vocabulary

Section 02 Conversation 1

Section 03 Conversation 2

Section 04 Conversation 3

Section 05 Saying Goodbye

Section 06 Review

Section 01

Vocabulary

- □ actual value: 실제가치
- □ actually better: 확실히 더 좋은
- □ charges: 요금
- □ circulation: 유통, 순환
- □ collector's item: 수집대상품
- □ commission: 수수료(커미션)
- □ commonly: 흔히, 보통
- □ continue: 계속하다
- □ coordinator: 조정자(코디네이터)
- □ currency: 통화
- □ eventually: 결국
- □ exchange: 교환, 교환하다
- □ expensive: 비싼
- □ increase: 증가하다, 인상하다
- □ instead: 대신에
- □ misunderstood: 오해를 받는
- □ monthly phone bill: 월 전화요금
- □ organize: 조직하다
- □ popular: 인기있는, 대중적인
- □ prefer: ~을 (더)좋아하다
- □ produce: 생산하다
- □ production costs: 생산비
- □ rarely: 드물게, 좀처럼 …하지 않는
- □ receipts: 영수증
- □ reduce: 줄이다, 축소하다, (가격 등을)낮추다
- □ salary: 급여, 봉급, 월급
- □ seldom: 좀처럼[거의] …않는
- □ sporting event: 스포츠 행사
- □ total cost: 총 비용

01 Pronunciation - Problem Numbers.

When using numbers it is important to pronounce them correctly. Below is a list of the most commonly mispronounced and misunderstood numbers. Practice your pronunciation of them.

• 12 Twelve – 20 Twenty	• 16 Sixteen – 60 Sixty
• 13 Thirteen – 30 Thirty	• 17 Seventeen – 70 Seventy
• 14 Fourteen – 40 Forty	• 18 Eighteen – 80 Eighty
• 15 Fifteen – 50 Fifty	• 19 Nineteen – 90 Ninety

02 Koreans and English speakers organize numbers differently. Many large Korean numbers are organized in groups of 10,000. In English many large numbers are organized in groups of 1,000.

Ex) 10,000 - ten thousand

Ex) 47,000 – forty seven thousand

Ex) 198,000 – one hundred ninety eight thousand

Try practicing the numbers listed below.

• 1 one	• 100,000 one hundred thousand
• 10 ten	• 1,000,000 one million
• 100 one hundred	• 10,000,000 ten million
• 1,000 one thousand	• 100,000,000 one hundred million
• 10,000 ten thousand	• 1,000,000,000 one billion

Section 02 Conversation 1

01 Listen to the following conversation and practice it with your partner.

Brandon: There are 800 people coming to the sporting event. What do we need to prepare?

Emily: We need to get 330 pizzas, 1600 hand towels, 3250 bottles of water, and 115 bags of ice.

Brandon: Ok that's 330 pizzas, 1600 hand towels, 3250 bottles of water, and 115 bags of ice.

Emily: These are your five assistants. You will work in teams of two. There are 3 delivery trucks. Pick up the items and be back here by 3:00 PM.

Brandon: Okay, teams let's go. We have a lot of work to do.

Emily: Drive safely!

브랜던: 스포츠 행사에 800명이 오기로 되어 있어요. 준비를 위해 무엇이 필요할까요?

에밀리: 피자 330, 손수건 1600, 물병 3250 그리고 아이스백 115개를 확보할 필요가 있어요.

브랜던: 좋아요. 피자 330, 손수건 1600, 물병 3250 그리고 아이스백 115개. 알겠어요.

에밀리: 이들은 당신의 5명의 보조원들이에요. 2인 1조로 일할 것이고요. 3대의 배달용 트럭이 있어요. 품목들을 선택해서 오후 3시까지 돌아오세요.

브랜던: 좋아요. 갑시다. 할 일이 많거든요.

에밀리: 안전운전하세요!

02 Try practicing more difficult numbers.

- 27,241: twenty seven thousand, two hundred forty one
- 3,650,000: three million, six hundred fifty thousand
- 19,900,000: nineteen million, nine hundred thousand
- 540,761,800: five hundred forty million, seven hundred sixty one thousand, eight hundred

03 Answer the questions with your teammates.

How many	Student 1	Student 2	Student 3
people are in your family?			
pairs of shoes do you own?			
computer games do you have?			

04 Money Practice.

Practice the prices in won.

- ₩10: ten won
- ₩100: one hundred won
- ₩1000: one thousand won
- ₩10,000: ten thousand won
- ₩100,000: one hundred thousand won
- ₩10,000,000: ten million won
- ₩50: fifty won
- ₩500: five hundred won
- ₩5000: five thousand won
- ₩50,000: fifty thousand won
- ₩1,000,000: one million won
- ₩100,000,000: one hundred million won

Practice the prices in dollars and cents.

- $ 0.01: one cent (penny)
- $ 0.05: five cents (nickel)
- $ 0.10: ten cents (dime)
- $ 0.25: twenty five cents (quarter)
- $ 0.50: fifty cents
- $ 1.00: one dollar
- $ 2.00: two dollars
- $ 5.50: five dollars, fifty cents/ five fifty
- $ 19.99: nineteen dollars, ninety nine cents/ nineteen ninety nine
- $ 99.95: ninety nine dollars, ninety five cents/ ninety nine ninety five
- $ 100: one hundred dollars

05 American Coins and Bills.

This is what American coins and bills look like.

1 penny/1 cent	1 nickel/5 cents	1 dime/10 cents	1 quarter/25 cents	1 dollar

$1	$2	$5

$10	$20	$50	$100

Section 03 Conversation 2

01 Listen to the following conversation and practice it with your partner.

Emily: Could you give me the prices on each of the items? I'd like to know the total cost for everything.

Brandon: Ok, 330 pizzas came to $4,950. 1,600 hand towels was $800. 3,250 bottles of water came to $1,625. And 115 bags of ice was $143.75.

Emily: All right. 4,950 plus 800 plus 1,625 plus 143.75 comes to a total of $7,518.75.

Brandon: Here are the receipts for everything.

Emily: Thank you, Brandon. I'll send them to the event coordinator right away.

에밀리: 각각의 품목에 대한 가격을 좀 알려 주시겠어요? 모든 품목에 대한 총비용을 알고 싶어요.
브랜던: 좋아요. 피자 330판 $4,950. 손수건 1,600장 $800. 물병 3,250 $1,625 그리고 아이스백 115개 $143.75 나왔습니다.
에밀리: 알겠습니다. 4,950, 800, 1,625, 143.75를 하게 되면 총 $7,518.75가 되군요.
브랜던: 여기 전 품목에 대한 영수증이 있어요.
에밀리: 고마워요. 그 품목들을 행사 코디네이터에게 곧 보낼께요.

02 Write the following numbers in English.

- 765,100 ______________________
- ₩1,690,000 ______________________
- ₩12,550,000 ______________________
- $1.95 ______________________
- 42,950,000 ______________________
- $119.99 ______________________
- $440,000,000 ______________________

03 Answer the questions with your teammates.

How much	Student 1	Student 2	Student 3
money do you have right now?			
did your smart phone cost?			
do you spend on coffee each week?			

04 Answer the following questions.

1. How much did your English textbook cost? ______________________
2. What does one U.S. dollar cost in Korean won? ______________________
3. How much is your monthly phone bill? ______________________
4. What do you like to spend money on? ______________________
5. What do you think is a good salary? ______________________
6. If you had a lot of money what would you buy? ______________________

Section 04 Conversation 3

01 Listen to the conversation and practice it with your partner.

Jacob: We need to exchange some money before we go shopping.

Samantha: I see two currency exchange places over there.

Jacob: The one on the left is offering a better rate. Let's go to that one.

Samantha: Wait a minute. The place on the left has a better rate but they also charge a 5% commission. That's 5 dollars on a hundred.

Jacob: The place on the right charges no commission, so the rate there is actually better.

Samantha: You're right, let's go to that place instead.

제이콥: 쇼핑하기전에 얼마의 환전이 필요해요.

사만타: 저쪽에 두 환전소가 있어요.

제이콥: 왼쪽의 환전소에서 더 좋은 환율이 제시되고 있어요. 그리로 가요.

사만타: 잠깐 기다려 봐요. 왼쪽에서는 더 좋은 환율이 제시되지만 5%의 커미션이 부과돼요. 백달러에 대해 5달러입니다.

제이콥: 오른쪽 환전소에서는 커미션이 부과되지 않아요. 그래서 그쪽 환율이 더 유리해요.

사만타: 좋아요. (왼쪽)대신 그곳으로 가요.

02 The Future of Money.

Sometimes money can be too expensive to produce. On February 4, 2013 the Royal Canadian Mint stopped producing the penny because it cost more to produce the coin than its actual value. The smallest unit of currency in Canada is now the five cent coin commonly known as the nickel. Prices in the country now end in zero or five, for example $9.90, $9.95, $10.00. The penny is still used in the United States, but as inflation and production costs increase over time they too will stop making the one cent coin. In South Korea the 10 won coin was reduced in size because it was expensive to produce. As production costs continue to go up, eventually the 10 won coin will be removed from circulation just like the penny was removed in Canada.

03 Answer the questions about the reading.

1. What is the problem that both the penny and the 10 won coin have?

____

2. How have prices in Canada changed?

____

3. What happened to the Canadian penny?

____

4. What happened to the Korean 10 won coin?

____

5. What happened to the American penny?

____

UNIT 05

Shopping

Section 01

Vocabulary

01 Practice your pronunciation of the following words and expressions.

- □ accepting: 쾌히 받아들이는, 솔직한
- □ advice: 충고, 조언, 권고
- □ affordable: 알맞은, 감당할 수 있는
- □ appearance: 모습, 외모, 나타남
- □ awesome: 경탄할만한, 엄청난
- □ borrowed: 빌린, 차용한
- □ cash payment: 현금지급
- □ compliment: 칭찬, 찬사, 인사
- □ congratulations: 축하, 경축
- □ convenience: 편의, 편리함
- □ debt: 빚, 부채
- □ discontinued: 중단된
- □ expired: 만료된
- □ fitting room: 탈의실
- □ footwear: 신발
- □ functions: 기능, 작용, 구실
- □ good fortune: 행운
- □ good taste (choice): 좋은 취향
- □ great job: 잘했어
- □ half price: 반값
- □ handle the payments: 결제를 처리하다
- □ handmade: 손으로 만든, 수제의
- □ homemade: 집에서 만든
- □ luxurious: 고급스런, 사치스런
- □ nice person: 좋은 사람
- □ obligation: 의무
- □ offer: 제의하다, 권하다
- □ opinion: 의견
- □ outfit: 채비, 용품, 의복
- □ permission: 허락, 허가
- □ personal information: 개인정보
- □ possibilities: 가능성, 가능한 일
- □ quality: 질(質)
- □ recommend: 추천하다, 권고하다
- □ regular price: 정가
- □ reliability: 신뢰할 수 있음, 신뢰, 확실성
- □ request: 요청, 요구
- □ tailor made: 맞춤의
- □ test drive: 시운전, 시승
- □ wardrobe: 옷장, (개인이 소유하고 있는)옷

Section 02 Conversation 1 – Modal Verbs

01 Listen to the conversation and practice it with your partner.

Tyler: There are two types of car I'm interested in, but I can't decide on which one to buy. Can you give me your opinion?

Emily: The red one looks really nice but it's more expensive.

Tyler: The blue one is cheaper. But it's not as luxurious as the red one.

Emily: I like the red one, but I think you'll be taking on too much debt if you buy it. I think you should buy the blue one.

Tyler: You're right Emily. I might not be able to handle the payments. I think I'll get the blue one.

Emily: It's only your first car. You can get a nicer one in the future.

타일러: 내가 관심을 갖는 2가지 유형의 자동차가 있어요. 그러나 어떤 자동차를 살지 결정할 수 없어요. 나에게 의견을 좀 줄래요.

에밀리: 붉은 자동차는 매우 좋아 보이지만 좀 더 비싸군요.

타일러: 푸른 자동차는 가격이 더 싸지만 붉은 자동차만큼 고급스럽지가 않군요.

에밀리: 붉은 것을 좋아해요. 그러나 당신이 그것을 구입하면 너무 많은 빚을 지게될 것으로 생각해요. 푸른색의 자동차를 구입하도록 해요.

타일러: 좋아요 에밀리. 내가 결제를 못할수도 있겠군요. 푸른색을 구입할까 해요.

에밀리: 당신의 첫번째 자동차예요. 장차 더 멋진 자동차를 구입할 수 있어요.

02 Modal Verbs.

Modal verbs indicate likelihood, ability, permission, and obligation. Modal verbs include **would, should, could, can, may, might, must, and will**. In shopping situations modal verbs can be used like the following:

- **Would**: offers and requests – Would you like to try on another size?
- **Should**: giving advice – You should keep the receipt in case you want a refund.
- **Could:** possibilities and requests – Could I exchange this item, please?
- **Can**: ability and permission – Can you deliver it by Friday?
- **May/Might**: possibilities – I might get a discount if I pay in cash.
- **Must**: obligation/requirement – To get a refund the item must be returned within 30 days.
- **Will**: requests – Will you let me take the car for a test drive?

To make a modal verb **negative** you should use **not** after the modal verb. You can also use its contraction, if there is one.

Ex) I **would not/wouldn't** recommend that type of phone.
Ex) You **should not/shouldn't** buy expired food.
Ex) We **could not/couldn't** return the item.
Ex) They **cannot/can't** accept cash payments.
Ex) She **may not** be here on time.
Ex) Customers **must not/mustn't** take more than three items into the fitting room.
Ex) We **will not/won't** find a better price than this.

03 Try making a sentence or question using each of the modal verbs.

1. (would) ____________________

2. (should) ____________________

3. (could) ____________________

4. (can) ____________________

5. (may) ____________________

6. (might) ____________________

7. (must) ____________________

8. (will) ____________________

04 Buying Things.

Work together with 3 other students and ask each other the following questions.

What kind of	Student 1	Student 2	Student 3
house would you like to buy?			
car would you like to buy?			
clothes do you want to buy?			
gift should you buy for your mother?			
food do you like to buy the most?			

Section 03 Conversation 2 - Shopping

01 Listen to the following conversation and practice it with your partner.

Salesperson: Can I help you with anything here?

Customer: Yes, I think I will take this pair of shoes.

Sales person: Ok, actually today we are having a 50% off sale on all brand name footwear. If you buy one pair of shoes at the regular price, you can get a second pair for 50% off.

Customer: A second pair of shoes for half price? That's a good deal. Ok, maybe I'll take a look around. My brother's birthday is next week.

Salesperson: The men's shoe section is over in aisles 7 to 10. If you need any help just let me know.

Customer: Thank you very much.

판매원: 제가 당신을 도울일이 있나요?

고객: 예. 이 신발을 사겠습니다.

판매원: 좋아요. 사실 오늘은 모든 신발에 대해 50% 할인판매를 하고 있어요. 만약 당신이 정가에 신발 한 켤레를 산다면, 두번째 신발은 50% 할인가에 구입할 수 있어요.

고객: 반값에 두번째 신발을요? 저렴하군요. 좋아요. 한번 둘러볼께요. 내 동생의 생일이 다음주거든요.

판매원: 남자신발섹션은 7-10 넘어에 있어요. 어떤 도움이 필요하면 알려주세요.

고객: 대단히 고맙군요.

02 Match the words to their meaning.

Words		Meanings
1. affordable	________	a. how much something costs
2. popular	________	b. what a product looks like
3. brand	________	c. how well a product works
4. convenience	________	d. the logo a company uses
5. price	________	e. how easy it is to use a product
6. reliability	________	f. produced at home and not in a factory
7. functions	________	g. clothing that is specially made for one customer
8. quality	________	h. how much people like something
9. appearance	________	i. no longer produced or sold
10. tailor made	________	j. the different uses a product has
11. discontinued	________	k. made by a person instead of a machine
12. handmade	________	l. reasonably priced; able to buy it
13. homemade	________	m. how well made a product is

03 Try making a sentence using each vocabulary word.

1. (affordable) ________________________________

2. (popular) ________________________________

3. (brand) ______________________________________

4. (convenience) ______________________________________

5. (price) ______________________________________

6. (reliability) ______________________________________

7. (functions) ______________________________________

8. (quality) ______________________________________

9. (homemade) ______________________________________

10. (tailor made) ______________________________________

11. (discontinued) ______________________________________

12. (handmade) ______________________________________

13. (appearance) ______________________________________

04 Talk About It.

Ask and answer the following questions with your partner.

1. What do you think is the most popular brand name of clothing?
2. How is the quality of that brand name clothing?
3. What kind of clothing is good to have tailor made?
4. What is your favorite homemade food?
5. What will you buy this weekend?
6. What is more important to you, price or brand name?

Section 04 Conversation 3

01 Listen to the following conversation and practice it with your partner.

Michael: That dress looks really nice on you.

Sarah: Thank you. It was a gift from my aunt.

Michael: Your aunt has good taste. Where did she get it?

Sarah: She bought it while she was on vacation in L.A. I might go to L.A. with her in the summer.

Michael: If you can, you should go. There are lots of places to go shopping and the prices are pretty good too.

Sarah: That is true, and I must update my wardrobe before school starts in the fall.

마이클: 드레스가 정말 당신에게 잘 어울리는군요.
사라: 고마워요. 숙모로부터 받은 선물이에요.
마이클: 당신 숙모는 좋은 취향을 갖고 있군요. 어디서 샀지요?
사라: 숙모가 L.A에서 휴가 중 그것을 샀어요. 나는 여름에 숙모와 함께 L.A에 갈지도 몰라요.
마이클: 가능하다면, 꼭 가세요. 쇼핑할 곳이 많고 가격 역시 매우 저렴해요.
사라: 사실이에요. 가을에 개학하기 전 내 옷을 업데이트 시켜야 해요.

02 Online Shopping.

Ask and answer the following shopping questions with your partner.

1. What is your favorite shopping website?
2. What do you like to buy online?
3. What is something you would not buy online?
4. Do you feel safe shopping online?
5. Why do so many people like online shopping?
6. Would you give your personal information to a website for a 30% discount?

03 Compliments.

Conversation Point!

Giving a compliment is a great way to open a conversation with other people. Compliments can be given for many things like clothing, appearances, hair styles, abilities, and even good fortune. Look at some of the examples of compliments given below and practice them.

- **Clothes**

· That's a great color on you.
· That sweater looks really nice on you.
· I love your dress.
· What a nice jacket.

Hair & Eyes

· You have great hair.
· You have beautiful eyes.
· I like your hairstyle.
· I really like your new hair color.
· Your new hairstyle makes you look younger.

Abilities

· You speak English very well.
· You have beautiful penmanship.
· You did a great job on the presentation.
· You played a great game.
· You play the piano beautifully.

>> Accepting a Compliment

Conversation Point!

When accepting a compliment most times people respond by saying **thank you** and then give **some small information**. Check the examples listed below.

1. That sweater looks really nice on you.
   — Oh, thank you. I bought it on sale yesterday.
2. What a nice jacket.
   — Oh, this old thing. I've had it for years.
3. That skirt is really pretty.
   — Thanks. I borrowed it from a friend.
4. I love your new hairstyle.
   — Thank you. I got it done last week.

Accepting compliments on abilities follows a similar pattern.

1. You did a great job on the presentation. — Thank you. I was so nervous.
2. You did very well on your exam. — Thank you. I studied very hard.
3. You played a great game. — Thanks, I've been playing for 10 years.
4. Nice job, Mr. Kim. — Thank you, sir.

>> Congratulations

Conversation Point!

Congratulating someone means to show your happiness for someone else's success or good fortune.

1. Congratulations on your new baby.
2. Congratulations on getting married.
3. Congratulations on your victory.
4. Congratulations on getting accepted to university.
5. Congratulations on your new job.
6. Congratulations. I'm very proud of you.

Accepting congratulations is very similar to accepting a compliment.

1. Congratulations on your team's victory.
   — Thank you. We really worked hard all season.
2. Congratulations on winning the lottery.
   — Thank you. I can't believe I won!
3. Congratulations on the new job.
   — Thank you. It's always been my dream to work here.

>> Review

Accept the compliments.

1. Wow I really like your sneakers. ______________________________

2. That outfit looks great on you. ______________________________

3. That shirt looks awesome. ______________________________

4. I like your new hairstyle. ______________________________

5. You look like you've lost weight. ______________________________

6. Congratulations on your new job. ______________________________

7. You girlfriend/boyfriend seems like a really nice person. ________________

8. I love your new car. ______________________________

9. Congratulations on winning the game. ______________________________

10. You did a great job. ______________________________

UNIT

06

Holidays, Seasons, and Weather

Section 01

Vocabulary

01 Practice your pronunciation of the following words and expressions.

- □ arid: 무미건조한
- □ blizzard: 눈보라
- □ breeze: 산들바람, 미풍
- □ calm: 잔잔한, 침착한
- □ cloudy: 구름이 낀, 흐린
- □ cold: 추운
- □ cool: 시원한, 서늘한
- □ crowded: 붐비는
- □ curious: 호기심이 많은
- □ damp: 축축한
- □ foggy: 안개가 낀
- □ freezing: 꽁꽁얼게 추운
- □ freezing rain: 얼어붙는 비
- □ frigid: 냉랭한, 추운
- □ hazy: 연무가 낀, 흐릿한
- □ heavy: 무거운
- □ home cooked: 가정에서 요리한, 손으로 만든
- □ humid: 습한
- □ humidity: 습도, 습기
- □ icy: 얼음같이 찬
- □ lanterns: 랜턴, 손전등
- □ liberation: 해방, 석방
- □ lunar: 달의
- □ mild: 가벼운, 순한
- □ misty: 안개가 낀, 자욱한
- □ moderate: 보통의
- □ overcast: 구름이 뒤덮힌, 음울한
- □ pleasant: 즐거운, 쾌적한
- □ precipitation: 강수, 강수량
- □ reservation: 예약
- □ smoggy: 스모그가 많은
- □ take off: 벗다, 이륙하다
- □ temperature: 온도, 기온
- □ temple: 신전, 사원, 관자놀이
- □ traditions: 전통
- □ warm: 따뜻한
- □ wind: 바람
- □ windy: 바람이 부는

>> Warm Up

1. Do you like to go shopping before big holidays like Chuseok and Seollal?
2. What kind of weather do you like to shop in?
3. On your last holiday, what was the weather like?

Section 02 Conversation 1 - Korean Holidays

01 Listen to the following conversation and practice it with your partner.

Chris: What is your favorite Korean holiday?

Jung Hoon: My favorite holiday is Chuseok.

Chris: Why do you like that holiday the most?

Jung Hoon: Chuseok is Korean Thanksgiving. I love eating a traditional home cooked meal and it's a three day holiday.

Chris: Nothing beats a home cooked meal. In my country Thanksgiving is just one day. Why is it a three day holiday in Korea?

Jung Hoon: Many people travel to their hometowns for Chuseok, so a three day holiday gives people more time to get together with their families and travel back home.

크리스: 당신이 가장 좋아하는 한국의 공휴일은 뭐예요?

정훈: 내가 가장 좋아하는 공휴일은 추석입니다.

크리스: 그 공휴일을 왜 가장 좋아하나요?

정훈: 추석은 한국의 추수감사절이거든요. 나는 집에서 만든 전통요리를 좋아해요. 그리고 3일간 쉬거든요.

크리스: 집에서 만든 요리보다 더 나은 것은 없어요. 우리나라에서는 추수감사절은 단 하루입니다. 왜 한국에서는 3일간의 공휴일이지요?

정훈: 많은 사람들은 추석을 보내기 위해 고향으로 갑니다. 그래서 3일간의 공휴일은 가족과 만나고 자기 집으로 되돌아 오는데 필요한 보다 많은 시간을 제공해 주기 때문입니다.

02 Korean Holidays.

Conversation Point!

Sometimes a foreigner may be curious about how Korean people celebrate different holidays. You can help them understand Korean culture by explaining what Korean people traditionally do on those days. Practice speaking about the Korean holidays listed below.

- **New Year's Day (January 1st)**

On New Year's Day many people like to go to the sea and mountains and watch the first sunrise of the year.

- **Seollal (Lunar New Year)**

It's a three day holiday in January or February. Family and relatives get together to honor their ancestors and bow to their family elders. Children who bow to their elders are often given money. Koreans like to eat traditional foods and many people like to have a bowl of rice cake soup called "tteokguk." In Korea a person's age is calculated by using the lunar calendar. So everyone in the country becomes one year older. The date for Seollal is different each year because it follows the lunar calendar.

- **Independence Movement Day (March 1st)**

This holiday celebrates Korea's declaration of independence from Japanese colonial rule and to remember those who died during the Japanese occupation.

- **Children's Day (May 5th)**

It's a holiday for children. People with kids are very busy on this day. Many Korean parents take their children to parks, toy stores and so forth. Lots of events are organized for children.

● **Buddha's Birthday**

Celebrates the birth of Buddha. Buddhist temples across the country like to hang lines of beautiful colored lanterns. The date of this holiday changes because it follows the lunar calendar.

● **Memorial Day (June 6th)**

This holiday is to honor the soldiers and people who have died for the country.

● **Liberation Day (August 15th)**

This holiday celebrates Korea's liberation from Japan in 1945.

● **Chuseok**

Chuseok is similar to Thanksgiving in America. It's a three day holiday where family and relatives get together to honor their ancestors and have a traditional meal together. Korean people eat a lot of rice cakes or songpyeon on this day. Chuseok follows the lunar calendar so the holiday may be in September or October.

● **National Foundation Day (October 3rd)**

This holiday celebrates the founding of the Korean nation by the first Korean named Dangun.

● **Hangeul Day (October 9th)**

Celebrates the invention of the Korean language and the creation of its written form by King Sejong.

Christmas (December 25th)

Christmas in Korea is similar to Christmas in many other countries but it's not as big a holiday as it is in the west.

03 Talking about Holidays.

Ask and answer the following questions with your partner.

1. What is your favorite Korean holiday?

2. Why do you like that holiday the most?

3. What do you like to do on that holiday?

4. When is the next Chuseok?

5. When is the next Seollal?

6. Do you like meeting your relatives on Seollal and Chuseok?

7. Where do you go to celebrate Chuseok?

8. How do you get there?

9. Which Korean holiday do you think foreigners would like the most? Why?

Section 03 Conversation 2 – Seasons and Weather

01 Listen to the following conversation and practice it with your partner.

Taylor: What do you think is the best season in Korea?

Keun Hyung: I think autumn is a really nice time of year.

Taylor: What is the weather like then? Is it very hot?

Keun Hyung: No, it's not as warm as the summer. The humidity drops and the wind keeps the sky clear.

Taylor: I hope I can see the trees changing color this fall. I hear it's really pretty out in the countryside.

Keun Hyung: On Hangeul Day I'm taking my girlfriend out to the countryside to take some pictures. You can join us if you like.

테일러: 당신은 한국에서 가장 좋은 계절은 무엇이라고 생각하시죠?

근형: 가을이 일년 중 정말 좋은 때라고 생각해요.

테일러: 그때 날씨는 어때요? 매우 덥나요?

근형: 아니오, 여름만큼 덥지 않아요. 습도는 떨어지고 바람으로 인해 맑은 하늘을 유지해요.

테일러: 이번 가을에는 색깔이 바뀌는 나무들을 보고싶어요. 시골지역에 나가보면 너무 아름답다고 듣고 있어요.

근형: 한글날 나의 여자친구를 시골로 데리고 가서 사진을 찍을까 해요. 괜찮다면 함께 가시죠.

02 Practice the different times of seasons.

winter	spring	summer	autumn/fall
early winter	early spring	early summer	early autumn/fall
mid-winter	mid-spring	mid-summer	mid-autumn/fall
late winter	late spring	late summer	late autumn/fall

03 Practice some of the weather related vocabulary.

- **Precipitation**: heavy snow, moderate snow, light snow, icy, freezing rain, light rain, moderate rain, heavy rain, foggy, misty, smoggy, humid, damp, dry
- **Wind**: light wind, moderate wind, strong wind, windy, calm, breeze
- **Sky**: sunny, cloudy, partly cloudy, hazy, clear, overcast
- **Temperature**: very hot, hot, warm, pleasant, mild, cool, cold, very cold, freezing

>> Explain what Korean weather is like in each part of each season.

Ex) In early summer it is hot and rainy.

1. (mid-summer) ______________________________
2. (late summer) ______________________________
3. (early autumn) ______________________________
4. (mid-fall) ______________________________
5. (late fall) ______________________________
6. (early winter) ______________________________
7. (mid-winter) ______________________________
8. (late winter) ______________________________

9. (early spring) ______________________________

10. (mid-spring) ______________________________

11. (late-spring) ______________________________

04 Read the passage and answer the questions that follow.

Welcome to the Seoul weather report. Today is Monday, June 16. The weather for today will be warm and sunny in the morning. However, by afternoon, clouds will roll in and the skies will become overcast. Expect light rain showers in the afternoon and heavy rainfall by evening. Temperatures will be around 26 degrees Celsius in the afternoon, but will cool off at night, dropping to 15 degrees Celsius. For the rest of the week expect more clouds and rain. But by next weekend it should be sunny and clear again.

Questions

1. What is the weather going to be in the morning? ______________________.
2. What's the weather going to be like in the afternoon? ______________________.
3. What's the weather going to be like in the evening? ______________________.
4. What's the temperature going to be in the afternoon? ______________________.
5. What's the temperature going to be like at night? ______________________.
6. What's the weather going to be like by the weekend? ______________________.

Section 04 Conversation 3

01 Listen to the following conversation and practice it with your partner.

Ashley: It's so hot here in the city. We should take off somewhere this weekend.

Jin Hee: We could go camping on the mountain or go to the beach if you want to get out of town for a couple of days.

Ashley: The beach sounds like a great idea. Which one do you recommend?

Jin Hee: I think we should go to the east coast. It's not as crowded and the water is cleaner.

Ashley: The holiday weekend is coming up so we better get our hotel room and bus tickets early.

Jin Hee: Good idea. I'll get on the computer and make a hotel reservation and buy our bus tickets.

에쉴리: 이 곳 도시는 매우 덥군요. 이번 주말에 어디론가 떠나야겠어요.

진희: 당신이 이틀정도 도시를 벗어나고 싶다면 산으로 캠핑을 가든지 또는 해변으로 갈 수 있어요.

에쉴리: 해변이 좋겠군요. 어떤 곳을 추천하세요?

진희: 동해안으로 가는 것이 좋겠는데요. 사람들이 붐비지도 않고 물도 깨끗하거든요.

에쉴리: 휴일 주말이 다가오니까 호텔방과 버스티켓을 일찍 구해야겠어요.

진희: 좋아요. 컴퓨터에 접속해서 호텔예약과 버스티켓을 구입할께요.

02 Put the activities in the box with the season they are usually done in.

go skiing	go swimming	prepare for Chuseok	plant crops
harvest crops	go to the beach	get a suntan	make a snowman
rake leaves	go skating	clean your house	watch flowers bloom

Summer	Fall	Winter	Spring
______	______	______	______
______	______	______	______
______	______	______	______

03 Seasonal Activities.

Answer the questions together.

What do you like to do for fun	Student 1	Student 2	Student 3
in the winter?			
in the summer?			
in the spring?			
in the fall?			

Section 05 Writing – Favorite Holiday

01 Write a paragraph about your favorite holiday.

• **Brainstorming – Write down some ideas for your story.**

My favorite holiday: ______________________________.

Date: ______________________________.

Where do I go: ______________________________.

What do I eat: ______________________________.

What do I drink: ______________________________.

Who do I meet: ______________________________.

Special ceremonies: ______________________________.

My favorite part: ______________________________.

• **Now write about your favorite holiday.**

My Favorite Holiday: ____________________

____

____

____

____

____

____

Section 06

Review

Match the holiday with the correct date.

Holiday		Date
1. Chuseok	_____	a. October 9
2. Christmas	_____	b. May 5
3. New Years	_____	c. Three days in January or February
4. Liberation Day	_____	d. January 1
5. Buddha's Birthday	_____	e. December 25
6. Children's Day	_____	f. October 3
7. Seollal	_____	g. One day in April or May
8. National Foundation Day	_____	h. Three days in September or October
9. Hangul Day	_____	i. June 6
10. Memorial Day	_____	j. August 15

UNIT 07

Food

Section 01 Vocabulary

Section 02 Conversation 1

Section 03 Conversation 2

Section 04 Conversation 3

Section 01 Vocabulary

- □ afraid: 두려워하는, 겁내는
- □ bake: 굽다
- □ bitter: 맛이 쓴
- □ bland: 부드러운, 담백한
- □ boil: 끓다
- □ brilliant idea: 훌륭한 생각
- □ burned: 불에 탄
- □ cabbage: 양배추
- □ celery: 셀러리
- □ cucumber: 오이
- □ deep fry: 기름에 튀기다
- □ delicious: 맛있는
- □ fast food: 패스트 푸드
- □ fermented: 발효된
- □ frozen: 냉동된
- □ fry: 기름에 튀기다
- □ greasy: 기름투성이의, 기름이 많이 묻은
- □ grill: 그릴, 석쇠
- □ ingredients: 성분, 요리의 재료
- □ lettuce: 레터스 상추
- □ medium: 약간의, 알맞게 익힌
- □ medium-rare: 약간 덜 익힌
- □ medium-well: 미디엄 웰던(잘 익힌)
- □ microwave: 전자렌지
- □ mushroom: 버섯
- □ overcooked: 너무 익힌
- □ rare: (스테이크가)덜 익은
- □ raw: 익히지 않은, 날것의
- □ reheated: 재가열된, 다시 데운
- □ roast: 굽다, 구운 고기
- □ roaster: 굽는 사람[기계]
- □ salad dressing: 샐러드용 드레싱
- □ salty: 짠, 소금기가 있는
- □ sauté: 살짝 볶은
- □ sesame oil: 참기름
- □ sour: 시큼한, 신
- □ spicy: 매운, 양념 맛이 강한
- □ stir fry: 프라이팬을 흔들면서 센불에 재빨리 익히다
- □ sweet: 단, 달콤한, 맛있는
- □ tear (paper): (종이를)찢다
- □ vegetables: 채소, 야채
- □ uncooked: 요리되지 않은, 날것의
- □ undercooked: 설익은
- □ well done: 고기가 잘 구워진(익힌)

Section 02 Conversation 1

01 Listen to the following conversation and practice it with your partner.

Austin: What should we have for dinner tonight?

Samantha: I defrosted a chicken, but I'm not sure what to make with it. How about fried chicken?

Austin: Fried chicken is too greasy. We should try a healthier way to cook it. Let's have roast chicken instead.

Samantha: That's a good idea. I love roast chicken. We can stuff the chicken with rice, dates, and ginseng.

Austin: That's a brilliant idea. I'll get the roaster out from the cabinet. This is going to be delicious.

Samantha: The chicken is all ready to go, so I will prepare the stuffing. After you get the roaster could you set the table please?

Austin: Sure. No problem.

오스틴: 오늘 저녁식사로 뭘 먹을까요?

사만타: 치킨을 해동시켰지만 그걸로 뭘 해야 할지 모르겠어요. 닭튀김은 어때요?

오스틴: 닭튀김은 너무 기름기가 많아요. 보다 몸에 좋은 요리 방식을 시도해야겠어요. 대신 로스트 치킨(통닭구이) 파티해요.

사만타: 좋은 생각이군요. 로스트 치킨을 좋아해요. 치킨에 쌀, 대추 그리고 인삼을 채워넣을 수 있어요.

오스틴: 훌륭한 생각이군요. 캐비네트에서 로스터를 꺼내 보겠어요. 맛이 있을 것 같군요.

사만타: 치킨은 시작할 준비가 되어 있으니 속 채우기를 준비할께요. 로우스터를 받은 후 식탁을 좀 차려 주실래요?

오스틴: 그러죠. 좋아요.

02 Look at the different ways to cook food.

microwave

roast

raw

sauté/fry

boil

steam

grill/barbecue

bake

deep fry

>> Using New Vocabulary

Write a sentence using the new vocabulary.

Ex) I will fry an egg for breakfast.

1. (grill) ______________________________
2. (bake) ______________________________
3. (deep fry) ______________________________
4. (steam) ______________________________

5. (boil) ______________________________

6. (sauté) ______________________________

7. (microwave) ______________________________

8. (raw) ______________________________

9. (roast) ______________________________

03 Stages of Food.

Practice the vocabulary and expressions describing stages of food listed below.

• undercooked	• medium-well	• reheated
• overcooked	• medium	• defrosted
• burned	• medium-rare	• frozen
• just right	• rare	
• well done	• uncooked	

04 Food Talk.

Answer the following questions and then talk with your partner.

1. What kind of food do you like to cook? ______________________________
2. How do you like your steak? ______________________________
3. What kind of food tastes better uncooked? ______________________________
4. What kind of frozen food do you like? ______________________________
5. What food doesn't taste good when it's reheated? ______________________________
6. What kind of food is very unhealthy? ______________________________

Section 03 Conversation 2

01 Listen to the following conversation and practice it with your partner.

Pizza Shop: Venice Pizzeria. How can I help you?

Min Su: Hi, I'd like to order a large pepperoni pizza and five small bottles of coke, please.

Pizza Shop: That's a large pepperoni pizza and five small bottles of coke. What is your address please?

Min Su: It's 1572 Jackson Street, apartment 302.

Pizza Shop: That's 1572 Jackson Street, apartment 302. Okay, it should be there in about 30 minutes.

Min Su: Thank you.

피자 가게: 뭘 도와 드릴까요?
민수: 안녕하세요. 페퍼로니 피자 큰 거 하나 하고 콜라 작은 걸로 5병 주문할께요.
피자가게: 페퍼로니 피자 큰 거 하나 그리고 콜라 작은 걸로 5병이군요. 주소를 알려주세요.
민수: 잭슨가 1572번지, 아파트 302호입니다.
피자가게: 잭슨가 1572번지, 아파트 302호이군요. 좋아요. 약 30분 후면 도착할 거예요.
민수: 고마워요.

02 Describing Tastes.

Practice the taste vocabulary listed below.

- spicy
- sweet
- strong
- greasy
- delicious
- salty
- sour
- bitter
- bland
- juicy

Tip

When describing tastes it helps to use words like **very**, **too**, and **a little bit** to explain the taste more clearly. Check the examples below.

Ex) Dakgalbi is very spicy.
Ex) The pizza is too salty.
Ex) Chinese food is a little bit greasy.

>> Put it Together

Use the words **very**, **too**, and **a little bit** to describe the tastes of foods.

1. (juicy) ______________________________

2. (delicious) ______________________________

3. (bland) ______________________________

4. (greasy) ______________________________

5. (strong) ______________________________

6. (sour) ______________________________

7. (sweet) ____

8. (salty) ____

9. (spicy) ____

03 Match the Korean foods with their descriptions.

Food Dish		Description
1. dakgalbi	_____	a. rice mixed with vegetables
2. ddukgook	_____	b. potato stew
3. hway	_____	c. raw fish
4. gamjatang	_____	d. spicy chicken and vegetable stir fry
5. kimchi	_____	e. sweet and sour pork
6. bibimbab	_____	f. boiled chicken stuffed with rice and ginseng
7. tangsooyook	_____	g. spicy fermented cabbage
8. samgyetang	_____	h. rice cake soup
9. goongoguma	_____	i. barbecued rib beef
10. galbi	_____	j. baked sweet potatoes

Section 04 Conversation 3

01 Listen to the following conversation and practice it with your partner.

Min Su: Let's get some lunch. What are you in the mood for?

Jacob: As long as it isn't fast food I'm ok. Maybe we should try some healthy Korean food.

Min Su: Sure, how about bibimbap? It's really good for you and it's not expensive either.

Jacob: I've never tried bibimbap before. What is it?

Min Su: It's rice and vegetables mixed in a bowl. You can add sesame oil and gochujung if you like it spicy.

Jacob: Spicy and healthy? That sounds perfect. I love spicy food.

민수: 점심먹어요. 무엇을 먹고 싶으세요?

제이콥: 패스트푸드가 아닌한 괜찮아요. 몸에 좋은 한국음식을 먹어보는 것도 좋겠군요.

민수: 좋아요. 비빔밥 어떠세요? 당신 건강에 매우 좋기도 하고 값도 비싸지 않아요.

제이콥: 나는 이전에 비빔밥을 먹어 본적이 없어요. 무슨 음식이죠?

민수: 볼(cup보다 깊고 큰 용기) 안에 쌀밥과 채소를 섞은 것이지요. 거기다가 참기름과 함께 매운맛을 좋아하면 고추장을 첨가할 수 있어요.

제이콥: 매운 맛과 건강? 그거 괜찮을 것 같네요. 매운 음식을 좋아해요.

02 Food Facts.

Conversation Point!

Sometimes there is no direct translation for some Korean foods in English. You must describe them instead. As you seen in the conversation there is no English word for bibimbap. Min Su had to explain what it was to Jacob.

Describe the following foods.

1. What is kimchi chigae? ______________________________
2. What is bulgogi? ______________________________
3. What is deagigalbi? ______________________________
4. What is bouldak? ______________________________
5. What is denjangchigae? ______________________________
6. What is samgyupsal? ______________________________

03 Talking About Korean Food.

1. What is your favorite Korean food? ______________________________
2. What Korean food does your mother make best? ______________________________
3. What Korean food do you dislike? ______________________________
4. What Korean food do you think foreigners like the most? ______________________________
5. What Korean food would foreigners be afraid to try? ______________________________

04 Reading a Recipe.

Complete the recipe using words from the box.

bowl	cucumber	tear	add	dressing	wash

______________ some tomatoes, lettuce, mushrooms, _______________, and celery.

Cut the vegetables and _____________ the lettuce into small pieces.

Put the cut vegetables into a large ____________.

_____________ your favorite salad _______________.

Mix the dressing with the vegetables and it's ready to serve.

05 Writing.

Write your favorite recipe for ramyeon. Include the ingredients and how to make it.

Recipe for Ramyeon

____

____

____

____

____

____

____

UNIT

08

Dates & Time

Section 01 Vocabulary

01 Practice your pronunciation of the following words and expressions.

- □ afternoon: 오후
- □ arrive: 도착하다
- □ begin: 시작하다
- □ exact time: 정확한 시간
- □ half past: …시 30분
- □ holiday: 공휴일
- □ in a few minutes: 수분 안으로
- □ lineup: 정렬
- □ midnight: 한밤중
- □ Parent's Day: 어버이날
- □ preposition: 전치사
- □ quarter after: …시 15분
- □ quarter past: …시 15분
- □ quarter to: …시 15분 전
- □ semester: 학기
- □ set period of time: 몇 기간 동안
- □ sleep in: 늦잠을 자다
- □ sunrise: 해돋이, 일출
- □ sunset: 일몰, 해질녘
- □ ticket booth: 매표소
- □ vacation: 휴가, 방학
- □ weekdays: 평일(월요일부터 금요일까지)

Section 02 Conversation 1 - Prepositions of Time

01 Listen to the conversation and practice it with your partner.

Michael: When do you wake up in the morning?

Jessica: I get up at 7 AM on weekdays.

Michael: What time do you arrive at work?

Jessica: I get to work at 9 AM.

Michael: Do you get up early on Saturday?

Jessica: No, that's my time to sleep in.

마이클: 아침 몇 시에 일어나세요?
제시카: 평일에는 오전 7시에 일어나요.
마이클: 일터에는 몇 시에 도착하나요?
제시카: 나는 오전 9시에 출근해요.
마이클: 토요일에 일찍 일어나나요?
제시카: 아니에요. 늦잠을 잘 수 있는 시간이에요.

02 Prepositions of Time.

The prepositions **on**, **in**, **at** are used when you speak about time. The preposition **on** is mostly used when you speak about **a day**.

Ex) on my birthday
Ex) on December 25th

Ex) on Saturday night

Ex) on Monday

The preposition **in** is mostly used for speaking about a **set period of time**.

Ex) in the afternoon

Ex) in July

Ex) in winter

Ex) in 2018

The preposition **at** is mostly used when speaking about an **exact time**.

Ex) at noon

Ex) at midnight

Ex) at 7 o'clock

Ex) at 5:35 AM

03 Write the correct prepositions.

1. ___________ September
2. ___________ Friday
3. ___________ sunrise
4. ___________ 1995
5. ___________ August 15th
6. ___________ 7 o'clock
7. ___________ Sunday morning
8. ___________ 9:05 PM
9. ___________ spring
10. ___________ Parents Day
11. ___________ the evening
12. ___________ January
13. ___________ the afternoon of July 1st
14. ___________ sunset
15. ___________ my mother's birthday
16. ___________ 30 minutes
17. ___________ night
18. ___________ a few minutes

04 Complete each of the time statements below.

1. ________________________________ on Saturday morning.
2. ________________________________ on my mother's birthday.
3. ________________________________ at night.
4. ________________________________ at 11:00PM.
5. ________________________________ in the afternoon
6. ________________________________ in the summer

Use **on**, **in** or **at** to complete the statements below.

7. I get to school ________________________________
8. On weekday mornings I usually wake up ____________________
9. My next vacation will start ________________________
10. I like to eat lunch ____________________________
11. I go to the beach ____________________________
12. The airplane will arrive ________________________

05 Talk about the following questions together with your classmates.

When will you go	Student 1	Student 2	Student 3
on vacation?			
home?			
meet your friends?			

Section 03

Telling Time

01 Practice the different ways to tell time.

	• twelve o'clock • noon • twelve PM • midnight • twelve AM
	• four fifteen (in the afternoon/PM) • four fifteen (in the morning/AM) • a quarter after four • a quarter past four
	• seven forty-five (in the morning/AM) • seven forty-five (in the evening/PM) • a quarter to eight
	• ten thirty (in the morning/AM) • ten thirty (at night/PM) • half past ten
	• six fifty (in the evening/PM) • six fifty (in the morning/AM) • ten to seven
	• nine oh five (in the morning/AM) • five after nine (in the evening/PM) • five past nine

02 Look at the clocks and write the correct time two different ways.

____

____

____

____

____

____

____

____

____

____

____

____

____

____

____

____

____

____

03 Practice some of these other useful time expressions.

We will meet **exactly at** 9:00AM

The show will begin at 2:00PM **sharp**.

We should be there by 8 o'clock **at the latest**.

We will work on the project **until** 10 PM.

Make sure you arrive there **before** noon.

She made it home **around** 9 o'clock.

04 Conversation 2.

Listen to the conversation and practice it with your partner.

Sung Min: Could you tell me the 509 bus schedule?

Ashley: The first bus arrives here at around 5 AM. The buses run until midnight.

Sung Min: Do you know when the next bus will arrive?

Ashley: If the traffic is ok, it should be here at 9 o'clock.

Sung Min: Oh good, I have to be at the airport by 11:00.

Ashley: Don't worry, after the bus leaves you will be at the airport in 20 minutes.

성민: 509호 버스 일정을 좀 알려 주세요.

에쉴리: 첫째 버스는 여기에 오전 5시경에 도착해요. 그 버스는 밤중까지 운행해요.

성민: 다음 버스는 언제 도착하는지 아세요?

에쉴리: 교통상황이 괜찮다면 9시에 도착할 거예요.

성민: 다행이군요. 11시까지 공항에 도착해야 하거든요.

에쉴리: 걱정말아요. 버스가 출발 후 20분 안으로 공항에 도착하게 될 거예요.

05 Answer the following questions.

1. When will you have dinner?

____

2. When did you eat breakfast today?

____

3. What day do you usually meet your friends?

____

4. What day do you have English class?

____

5. When is the best time to visit Jeju Island?

____

6. When is the Winter Olympics in Korea?

____

Section 04

Months and Dates

01 Practice the months and the dates below.

Months					
January	February	March	April	May	June
July	August	September	October	November	December

Dates					
1st	first	**12th**	twelfth	**23rd**	twenty-third
2nd	second	**13th**	thirteenth	**24th**	twenty-fourth
3rd	third	**14th**	fourteenth	**25th**	twenty-fifth
4th	fourth	**15th**	fifteenth	**26th**	twenty-sixth
5th	fifth	**16th**	sixteenth	**27th**	twenty-seventh
6th	sixth	**17th**	seventeenth	**28th**	twenty-eighth
7th	seventh	**18th**	eighteenth	**29th**	twenty-ninth
8th	eighth	**19th**	nineteenth	**30th**	thirtieth
9th	ninth	**20th**	twentieth	**31st**	thirty-first
10th	tenth	**21st**	twenty-first		
11th	eleventh	**22nd**	twenty-second		

02 Conversation 3.

Listen to the conversation and practice it with your partner.

Sara: I got five tickets for the concert in June.

Kyung Mi: I can't believe you got tickets. They went on sale at noon on Tuesday, but the ticket website crashed and I couldn't buy them.

Sara: I was afraid that would happen, so I waited in line at the ticket booth.

Kyung Mi: The concert was sold out in an hour. When did you get in the lineup?

Sara: I got in the lineup yesterday at around 9:00AM. You can have one of my tickets. Just give me the money for it on payday.

Kyung Mi: Thank you so much Sara. You're the best.

사라: 6월 콘서트의 티켓 5장을 구입했어요.
경미: 티켓을 구입했다는 걸 믿을 수가 없군요. 티켓은 화요일 정오에 판매되기 시작했지만 티켓 웹사이트의 갑작스런 문제로 인해 티켓을 구입할 수가 없었어요.
사라: 그러한 일이 발생할까봐 걱정했거든요. 그래서 매표소에서 줄을 서서 기다렸지요.
경미: 그 콘서트의 티켓은 한 시간만에 매진되었어요.
사라: 어제 오전 9시 경에 줄을 섰어요. 내 티켓 중 한 장을 가져도 돼요. 티켓값은 급여일에 주세요.
경미: 고마워요 사라. 당신이 최고예요.

03 Answer the following questions.

1. When is your birthday? ______________________________

2. When does the school semester finish? ______________________________

3. When is Christmas? ______________________________

4. When is your next English class? ____________________

5. When is your next holiday? ____________________

04 Use time expressions or dates and times together in your answers.

Ex) When was your club meeting? — A. It was on Monday evening at 7:00.

1. When is your next English class?

____

2. When is your first class next week?

____

3. When is your final exam for English?

____

4. When exactly will your next vacation start?

____

5. When is your major class each week?

____

UNIT

09

Entertainment

Section 01

Vocabulary

- □ athlete: 운동선수
- □ cancel: 취소하다
- □ check it out: 확인하다, 알아보다
- □ combine: 결합하다
- □ created: 창작된
- □ famous musician: 유명한 음악가
- □ gratitude: 감사
- □ immediately: 즉시
- □ instead of: ~대신에
- □ invite: 초대[초청]하다
- □ invitation: 초대
- □ likely: ~할 것 같은
- □ music collection: 음악소장〈수집〉
- □ musical instrument: 악기
- □ movie character: 영화에 나오는 캐릭터
- □ movie opening: 영화 개봉
- □ obsession: 집착, 강박관념
- □ opinion: 의견
- □ posters (paper): (종이)포스터
- □ primarily: 주로
- □ refusing: 거부하는, 싫어하는
- □ romantic: 낭만적인
- □ scholarship: 장학금, 학문
- □ slasher film: 슬래셔 영화
- □ sporting venue: 스포츠 경기 장소
- □ take a look: ~을 보다

Section 02 Conversation 1 - Sports

01 Listen to the following conversation and practice it with your partner.

Matthew: What do you like to do in your free time?

Sarah: I like to play computer games, watch movies, and sometimes Skype with my friends. What are you into?

Matthew: I like to play computer games and watch movies too. I have a slight obsession with playing basketball. I practice every day. I hope I can be good enough to get a scholarship.

Sarah: Cool. What team do you play on?

Matthew: I play on a team called the Rockets. We play our next game tomorrow night in the school gymnasium at 8:00PM. You should come check it out.

Sarah: Thanks for the invite. I think I'll drop by and take a look after class.

매튜: 한가한 시간에는 어떤 일을 즐겨하세요?

사라: 컴퓨터 게임, 영화보기 그리고 가끔 친구들과 스카이프 서비스를 이용해 인터넷 상에서 음성 대화를 나누기 좋아해요. 당신은 뭐에 관심 있으세요?

매튜: 나 역시 컴퓨터 게임과 영화보기를 좋아해요. 나는 농구경기에 약간의 강박관념을 갖고 있어요. 나는 매일 연습해요. 장학금을 받을 자격이 있으면 좋겠네요.

사라: 멋지군요. 어떤 팀에서 운동하세요?

매튜: 로켓이라고 부르는 팀에서 운동해요. 다음 경기는 학교 체육관에서 내일 밤 8시에 있어요. 와서 확인해 보세요.

사라: 초청해 주어서 감사해요. 방과 후에 들러서 볼까해요.

02 Talking About Sports.

Answer the following sports questions.

1. What kind of summer sports do you like?

____

2. What kind of sports did you play in high school?

____

3. What kind of winter sports do you like?

____

4. Who is the most famous athlete in South Korea?

____

5. Who is the most famous athlete in the world?

____

6. What sports will you check out at the 2018 Winter Olympics?

____

Tip

Sport English Fact

The word **soccer** is a word that is primarily used by only Americans and Canadians. Most people use the word **football** when talking about the sport. If you use the word **football** with Americans, for example, they will think you are talking about **American football**. If you speak with someone from outside North America they most likely will use the word **football** instead of **soccer**.

03 Sporting Venues.

Types of Sporting Venues		
arena	gymnasium	ice rink
baseball field	basketball court	stadium
soccer pitch/field	golf course	tennis court

04 Discuss these questions with your partner.

1. Where is the best place to watch a live sports event?
2. What is good about that place?
3. Which famous teams or athletes play there?
4. Is that place far away from here?
5. What is the best way to travel to that place?

Section 03 Conversation 2 - Music

01 Listen to the following conversation and practice it with your partner.

Hannah: Do you have a large music collection?

Nick: I have a huge music collection. When I hear a song I really like I download it immediately.

Hannah: I like to buy DVDs about my favorite musicians and music groups. I want to know everything about them and their music. Do you pay for the music you download?

Nick: Oh, of course. It doesn't cost that much. If a singer or music group I like comes to town, I always buy a ticket and go see them live. At the concerts I like to buy t-shirts, posters, and other cool stuff they have on sale.

Hannah: So are there any good singers or music groups coming here soon?

Nick: There are a couple of good concerts coming up next month. I am going to go see them both.

한나: 당신은 음악 수집물이 상당하지요?

닉: 음악 수집물이 엄청나요. 내가 노래를 듣다가 정말 좋아하면 즉시 다운로드 받아요.

한나: 내가 좋아하는 뮤지션과 뮤직그룹의 DVD 구입을 좋아해요. 뮤지션과 그들의 음악에 관한 모든 것을 알고 싶어요. 다운로드 받는 음악에 요금을 지불하나요?

닉: 물론이죠. 그렇게 많이 들지는 않아요. 만약 내가 좋아하는 가수나 뮤직그룹이 시내에 오면, 나는 항상 티켓을 구입해서 라이브로 그들을 보러가요. 콘서트에서 티셔츠, 포스터 그리고 그들의 판매하는 여타 멋진 것을 구매하기를 좋아해요.

한나: 괜찮은 가수 또는 뮤직 그룹이 이곳에 머지 않아 오나요?

닉: 다음달 2차례의 괜찮은 콘서트가 있어요. 둘 다 모두 가서 볼 거예요.

02 Music Vocabulary.

There are so many different types of music. The more common types of music are listed below.

pop music	jazz	R&B
K-pop	hip hop music	gospel music
rock music	dance music	theme music
classic rock	country music	soundtrack music
classical music	traditional music	children's music

Tip

In America many English words evolve and change over time. This is quite common in popular culture. Americans especially like to combine two word expressions into shorter expressions. For example expressions like **electronic mail** were combined to form the word **email**, **situation comedy** was shortened into the word **sitcom**, **science fiction** was shortened to **sci–fi**, and **rhythm and blues** was shortened into **R&B**. Since old words disappear and new ones are created, top English students should always stay up to date on the changes.

03 Answer the following questions about music.

1. What kind of music do you like?

___

2. Who is the most popular music group in Korea right now?

___

3. Have you ever seen a concert by a famous singer or band?

____

4. How often do you go see live concerts?

____

5. What is the best place to see live music in Seoul?

____

6. Can you play a musical instrument?

____

7. Do you like turot music?

____

04 Talking About Music.

Make a group of three people and discuss the following questions together.

1. If you could meet a famous musician or singer, who would you want to meet?
2. Did your parents pressure you to take music classes when you were young?
3. Do you usually download music from the internet without paying for it?
4. What kind of music do your parents like?
5. Why do so many Koreans go to Europe and America to study music?

Section 04 Conversation 3 - Movies

01 Listen to the conversation and practice it with your partner.

Girlfriend: There is a new Tom Cruise movie opening in the theater tonight. Let's go see it.

Boyfriend: How about I just download it and we can watch it at home? We can save money that way.

Girlfriend: But seeing it in the theater is so much better. I love seeing a movie on the big screen, the sound is better there, and it's more romantic.

Boyfriend: Ok, I guess so. What time does it start?

Girlfriend: It starts at 8:00PM. Get your jacket and come on, lets' go.

여자친구: 오늘 밤 극장에서 개봉되는 톰크루즈 영화가 있어. 가서 보자.

남자친구: 내가 그것을 다운로드 받아서 집에서 보는 게 어때? 돈을 절약할 수 있잖아.

여자친구: 그렇지만 극장에서 영화를 보는 것이 훨씬 더 좋아. 대형 스크린을 통해 영화 보는 것을 좋아하는데 음향도 더 좋고 보다 낭만적이야.

남자친구: 좋아. 나도 그렇게 생각해. 몇 시에 시작하지?

여자친구: 오후 8시에 시작해. 재킷을 챙겨입고와. 가자.

02 Using Let's.

The word **let's** can be used to invite someone to do something together. Make sentences using **Let's + verb**.

Ex) Let's watch that new television program.

Complete the sentences below.

1. Let's go ____________________
2. Let's play ____________________
3. Let's eat ____________________
4. Let's take ____________________
5. ____________________ a movie together.
6. ____________________ a trip to Vancouver.
7. ____________________ to a night club tonight.
8. ____________________ for our English exam.

03 Movie Vocabulary.

Below are the different types of movies

drama	thrillers	animation	romance
comedy	slasher	documentary	romantic comedy
action	sci-fi	musical	mystery
war movie	adventure	comedy drama	fantasy
horror	sports	crime drama	

04 Talking About Movies.

Answer the questions about movies together with your partner.

1. What kind of movies do you like? ______________________________

2. What kind of movies do you dislike? ______________________________

3. Who is your favorite foreign actor/actress? ______________________________

4. Who is your favorite Korean actor/actress? ______________________________

5. Do you prefer books or movies? ______________________________

6. What is your favorite movie theater? ______________________________

7. When is it more expensive to buy a ticket at the theater? ______________________________

8. When is it cheaper to buy a ticket at the movie theater? ______________________________

9. What is the best movie membership card to have? ______________________________

10. What kind of snacks do you eat at the movie theater? ______________________________

05 Use the words in the box to complete the conversation.

7:00 PM	busy	you then	you like to	movie	want to
how about	shall	Central CGV	boring	have in mind	

A: Say, are you ______________________ this weekend?

B: No, what do you __________________________?

A: Would ____________________________________ go to a movie with me?

B: Sure, sounds great. What _______________ do you _________________see?

A: ______________________ the new sci-fi movie?

B: Nah. I heard it's really _________________________.

A: Well, why not the new James Bond movie?

B: Great idea. When _____________________ we meet?

A: How about at ___________________ at __________________ on Saturday?

B: Ok. See ______________________.

06 Talking About Movies.

Make a team of three people and ask each other the questions below.

1. Where do you like to sit in the movie theater?
2. What movie have you seen recently? What is your opinion of that movie?
3. What do you find annoying at the movie theater?
4. If you could be a movie character, who would you be?
5. Do you like seeing 3D and 4D movies?

Section 05 Making Plans

01 Making Plans.

If you want to make plans to do something with others you can use the expressions below.

Ex) **Do you have any plans** for the weekend/on Saturday?
Ex) **Would you like to go** to the movies on Friday?
Ex) **Do you want to** come over for dinner tomorrow evening?

Accepting

Ex) I'd love to.
Ex) That sounds great/awesome/fun/nice.
Ex) Sure.

Refusing and Giving Excuses

Ex) I'd love to, but I'm going hiking.
Ex) Sorry, I'm going to my sister's house then.
Ex) That sounds great/awesome/nice/fun, but I have to work.
Ex) I'm afraid I'll be busy then.
Ex) I'm sorry, I already have plans.

You can also show your gratitude for the invitation by saying:

Ex) I'd love to, but I'm going hiking. **But thanks for asking.**
Ex) Sorry, I'm going to my sister's birthday party then. **Maybe next time.**

Speaking Practice

Try inviting your partner to do something. Practice accepting or refusing the invitation.

1. Do you have any ______________________________?
2. Would you like to______________________________?
3. Do you want to ______________________________?

02 Canceling a Plan.

You can cancel a plan by saying the following:

Sorry but I have to cancel our plans because I am feeling really sick today.
Sorry, but I forgot that I'd already made plans to help my little brother study for his math exam.

Accepting

Accept a canceled plan like this:

That's alright.
I understand.
No problem.
That's too bad.
Maybe next time.

UNIT

10

The Future

Section 01

Vocabulary

□ anywhere: 어디에, 어디든

□ beautiful: 아름다움

□ cancelled: 취소된

□ charged (battery): 충전된(배터리)

□ convenience store: 편의점

□ dream job: 이상적인 직업

□ envious: 부러워하는, 선망하는

□ expect: 예상하다

□ frustrating: 불만스러운, 좌절감을 주는

□ go on a date: 데이트 하러 가다

□ graduating: 졸업하는

□ hometown: 고향

□ hope: 바라다, 희망하다

□ job application: 구직

□ koala bear: 코알라

□ last minute: 막바지의

□ looking forward to: ~을 기대하다

□ part time job: 시간제일

□ raise your children: 아이들을 키우다

□ retire: 은퇴하다

□ someday: 언젠가

□ sounds like fun: 재미있을 것 같다

□ quickly: 빨리

□ waterfall: 폭포

Section 02 Conversation 1

01 Listen to the following conversation and practice it with your partner.

Michael: What will you do this summer?

Jung Hoon: I am going to get a part time job.

Michael: What kind of part time job are you going to get?

Jung Hoon: I will try to find a job working in a restaurant or a coffee shop. What are you going to do this summer?

Michael: I will be getting a part time job, too. I am going to work in my uncle's convenience store.

Jung Hoon: I envy you. It's good that you won't have to search around for a job.

마이클: 이번 여름에 무슨 일을 할 건가요?

정훈: 시간제 일자리를 구할 계획입니다.

마이클: 어떤 시간제 일자리를 구할 계획인가요?

정훈: 레스토랑이나 커피숍에서 일하는 일자리를 구해 보려고 해요. 당신은 이번 여름에 무슨 일을 할 계획인가요?

마이클: 나 역시 시간제 일을 구할 생각입니다. 삼촌의 편의점에서 일할 계획으로 있어요.

정훈: 당신이 부럽군요. 일자리를 찾으러 돌아다니지 않아도 되어 좋겠군요.

02 The Future Tense with Will & Going To.

Two common expressions for talking about the future are **will** and **going to**. They basically have the same meaning in the future tense. Check the examples below.

will + verb	going to + verb
I **will** fill out a job application. My friend **will** get a part time job soon. She **will** buy fruit for her father.	I am **going to** fill out a job application. My friend is **going to** get a part time job soon. She is **going to** buy fruit for her father.

To use **will** and **going to** in the negative form you can use the expressions **not going to**, **will not**, or **won't**. Check the examples below.

will not/won't + verb	not going to + verb
He **will not** change his phone number. They **will not** be there very long. You **won't** have to work on Monday	He is **not going to** change his phone number. They are **not going to** be there very long. You are **not going to** have to work on Monday.

03 Complete the sentences using a verb.

Ex) You will see a beautiful waterfall.

Ex) It is going to happen very quickly.

1. I will ______________________________

2. You are going to ______________________________

3. She will not ______________________________

4. He is not going to ______________________________

5. It won't ______________________________

6. They are not going to ______________________________

7. We are going to ______________________________

>> Make questions using will and going to.

Ex) Are you going to go home soon?

1. (going to) ______________________________?

2. (will) ______________________________?

3. (won't) ______________________________?

4. (not going to) ______________________________?

04 Future Time Expressions.

later today	tomorrow afternoon	this weekend
later this evening	tomorrow evening	next week
tonight	tomorrow night	a week from today
tomorrow	the day after tomorrow	two weeks from today
tomorrow morning	this Thursday	next September
in 5 minutes/five minutes from now	shortly	sooner or later
in 2 days	in the future	
in a year	in a little while	
soon	eventually	

Complete the sentences.

1. ________________________________ tomorrow.
2. ________________________________ this Saturday.
3. ________________________________ sooner or later.
4. ________________________________ shortly.
5. ________________________________ the day after tomorrow.

Complete the sentences using future time expressions.

1. I am going to eat dinner ________________________________.
2. I will buy a new phone ________________________________.
3. I will meet my friends ________________________________.
4. I am not going to go shopping ________________________________.
5. I will not take a trip ________________________________.

05 Speaking Practice.

Answer the following questions with your teammates.

What will you	Student 1	Student 2	Student 3
do on the weekend?			
eat for dinner tonight?			
do on your next vacation?			

Section 03 Conversation 2

01 Listen to the following conversation and practice it with your partner.

Tyler: I wish I could buy a new phone.

Samantha: It looks fairly new. What's wrong with it?

Tyler: This one will not work well with certain apps. It's really frustrating.

Samantha: I want to get a new phone, too. Mine is old and the battery won't stay charged for very long.

Tyler: I expect to get a new phone next month. Would you like to go shopping for a phone with me?

Samantha: Sure, that sounds like fun. I'm looking forward to it.

타일러: 내가 새로운 전화기를 살 수 있으면 좋을텐데.
사만타: 아주 새것으로 보이는데. 무슨 문제라도 있어요?
타일러: 어떤 앱(애플리케이션 프로그램)에서는 잘 작동이 안돼요.
사만타: 나 역시 새 전화기를 구입하고 싶어요. 내 것은 오래되었고 배터리 충전이 오래가지 않아요.
타일러: 나는 다음 달에 새 전화기 구입을 기대하고 있어요. 나와 같이 전화기 사러 갈까요?
사만타: 좋아요. 재미있을 것 같은데요. 정말 기다려지는데요.

02 Talk about the Future.

There are other expressions you can use to talk about the future. You can use words like **want to, wish, hope, expect, and look forward to**.

Ex) Min Su wants to be a doctor in the future.

Ex) I wish my boyfriend had some more vacation time this summer.

Ex) I hope my old battery charger will fit my new phone.

Ex) I expect her here in a few minutes.

Ex) We look forward to seeing you again.

>> Writing Practice

Make sentences using the following words.

1. (want to) ____________________

2. (wish) ____________________

3. (hope) ____________________

4. (expect) ____________________

5. (look forward to) ____________________

You can use the word **would** to talk about possible activities in the future.

Ex) I would love to have some ice cream.

Ex) I would visit Florida if I had the money.

>> Writing Practice

Answer the following questions using the word **would**.

1. What would you like to change about your home? ______________________
2. What would you like to buy? ______________________
3. What would you do if you won the lottery? ______________________
4. Where would you like to fly to? ______________________
5. Who would you like to go on a date with? ______________________

03 Time Traveler.

Try using the expression would in the speaking exercise below together with your partner.

A time machine has been invented. You can go to the past or the future.

1. What year do you want to go to? — I would go to the year ______________________
2. Where do you want to go? — I would go to ______________________
3. What will you do there? — I would ______________________

Section 04 Conversation 3

01 Listen to the following conversation and practice it with your partner.

Sun Hee: I am going to take a trip to Australia this winter. My dad said he will give me the money to go.

Min Su: That is awesome. I wish I could go to Australia. So, what will you do there?

Sun Hee: I'm going to Sydney so I am expecting to see the opera house, and I want to take a picture with a koala bear and a kangaroo.

Min Su: I'm so envious. I won't be going anywhere this winter except to my part time job.

Sun Hee: When will you start working?

Min Su: Right after final exams. It pays pretty well, so I am kind of looking forward to it.

선희: 이번 겨울에 호주로 여행을 할려고 해요. 아버지께서 여행할 돈을 나에게 주시겠다고 하셨어요.
민수: 멋지군요. 나도 오스트레일리아 갈 수 있으면 좋겠어요. 그래, 거기서 무엇을 할 예정인가요?
선희: 시드니로 가서 오페라 하우스를 볼 예정이예요. 그리고 코알라와 캥거루와 함께 사진 찍고 싶어요.
민수: 부럽군요. 나는 이번 겨울에 시간제 일을 제외하고는 아무데도 갈 수가 없어요.
선희: 언제 일을 시작하게 되나요?
민수: 기말고사가 끝나고 바로예요. 수입이 꽤 좋아서 나는 좀 기대하고 있어요.

02 Future Talk.

Answer the questions together with your partner.

1. Is there anything you are looking forward to?

____

2. What kind of job do you hope to have someday?

____

3. What do you wish you could do?

____

4. What is something you looked forward to that was cancelled at the last minute?

____

5. If you could have three wishes, what would you wish for?

____

03 In the Future.

You can use the expression **in the future** at the start of your sentence to talk about future plans, actions or events.

Ex) In the future, I will be a pro gamer.
Ex) In the future, I am going to travel the world.

Use the expression "in the future" to answer the following questions with your partner.

1. In the future, where do you want to live? ______________________________

2. In the future, when do you want to get married? __________________________

3. In the future, when do you want to have children? ________________________

4. In the future, where do you want to retire? ______________________________

5. In the future, how old will you be when you retire? ________________________

04 Speaking Practice.

Make a team of 3 students. Ask and answer the questions together.

In the future	Student 1	Student 2	Student 3
what kind of person do you want to marry?			
would you move back to your hometown?			
where do you want to raise your children?			

05 Using After.

You can use the expression "after" to talk about future activities that will start when another action finishes.

Ex) After graduation I will take a trip to Canada with my friends.

Ex) After class I am going home to get some sleep.

Complete the following sentences.

1. After getting my dream job ____.

2. After dinner tonight ____.

3. After my last exam ____.

4. After graduating ____.

5. After getting married ____.

UNIT 11

Frequency & Count Words

Section 01 Vocabulary
Section 02 Conversation 1
Section 03 Conversation 2
Section 04 Conversation 3
Section 05 Review

Section 01 Vocabulary

□ barrel: 배럴, 한 통의 양

□ bouquet: 부케, 꽃다발

□ bucket: 양동이, 들통

□ carton: 곽[통], 한 곽

□ catch up on: ~을 따라잡다

□ eat out: 외식하다

□ flock: (양, 염소, 새의)떼

□ keg: 작은 통

□ loaf: 한 덩어리의 빵

□ ounce: 온스

□ swarm: 떼(무리), 벌떼

□ tub: 통(뚜껑이 없고 둥글게 생긴 큰 것)

□ uncountable: 셀 수 없는(불가산의)

Section 02 Conversation 1

01 Listen to the conversation and practice it with your partner.

Brandon: How often do you meet your girlfriend?

Min Su: I usually meet her about once a week. This week I will meet her on Friday. It's her birthday.

Brandon: I guess you will have to buy her a gift. What will you get her?

Min Su: For any special day I always buy her a bouquet of flowers, and maybe a box of chocolates and a bottle of wine.

Brandon: I think she will like that. Do you plan to go out to see a movie?

Min Su: We go to the theater quite often, so I think I will do something different this time.

브랜든: 당신은 여자친구를 얼마나 자주 만나나요?

민수: 나는 보통 일주일에 한번 만나요. 이번 주에는 금요일에 만나려고 해요. 여자친구의 생일이거든요.

브랜든: 당신은 여자친구에게 선물을 해야할 것 같군요. 그녀에게 무엇을 사줄 건가요?

민수: 어떤 특별한 날에는 나는 항상 꽃다발과 그리고 초콜릿 한 상자와 와인 한 병 정도를 그녀에게 사주어요.

브랜든: 그녀가 좋아하겠군요. 영화보러 외출할 계획이 있어요?

민수: 우리는 꽤 자주 영화관에 가는 편이어서 이번에는 다른 뭔가를 할려고 해요.

02 Adverbs of Frequency.

Use adverbs of frequency to talk about how often you do something. The most commonly used adverbs of frequency are **always, usually, often, sometimes, seldom,** and **never**. They almost always go in the second position after the subject. Check the examples below.

Ex) I **always** meet my friends on the weekend.

Ex) We **usually** have a bowl of rice and soup for breakfast.

Ex) He **often** buys a box of oranges when he goes to Jeju Island.

Ex) She **sometimes** drinks a cup of tea after dinner.

Ex) They **never** show up late for class.

03 Use the following adverbs in a sentence.

1. (always) ____________________

2. (usually) ____________________

3. (often) ____________________

4. (sometimes) ____________________

5. (seldom)____________________

6. (never) ____________________

04 Match the adverbs with the time expressions.

	always	usually	often	sometimes	seldom	never
1. every night						
2. once a month						
3. once a year						
4. not at all						
5. once every 3 weeks						
6. 4 times a month						
7. every Saturday						
8. once a week						

05

There are many ways to answer the question **"How often do you _____?"** Below are some other examples of expressions you can use to answer this question. All of these words and phrases except **"never"**, go at the end of a sentence.

3 times a day	once a day	almost never
a lot	once a month	never
every hour	once a year	from time to time
every day	all the time	once in a while
once a week	only on Wednesday	

Make a team of 3 people and ask each other the following questions.

How often do you	Student 1	Student 2	Student 3
download TV shows?			
listen to music?			
cook?			
call your parents?			
exercise?			
eat pizza?			
drive a car?			
meet your friends?			

06 Complete the sentences using adverbs of frequency.

1. I ______________________________ eat Mexican food.

2. I ______________________________ upload pictures to the Internet.

3. I ______________________________ play sports.

4. My best friend usually ______________________________.

5. My mother always ______________________________.

07 How Much Time.

Talk to your partner about the following questions.

a. How much time does it take you to________?

1. go from home to school
2. eat lunch
3. check your e-mail
4. read a book
5. do your homework
6. cook ramyeon

Ex) It takes me 30 minutes to eat lunch.

b. How much time do you spend each day _____?

1. sleeping
2. watching TV
3. using the Internet
4. exercising
5. studying in class
6. playing games

Ex) I spend six hours a day sleeping.

Section 03 Conversation 2

01 Listen to the conversation and practice it with your partner.

Emily: What should we order for dessert?

Hannah: I think I'm going to have a piece of cake and a cafe latte. How about you?

Emily: I going to have a slice of cheese cake and a bottle of coke.

Hannah: I've changed my mind. I think I'm going to eat healthy and have a piece of fruit instead.

Emily: That's a good idea. I think I'll have something healthy, too. I'm going to have a cup of green tea.

Hannah: We should be more careful about what we eat.

에밀리: 디저트로 뭘 주문할까요?
한나: 케이크 한 조각과 함께 카페라테 한 컵을 마실려고 해요. 당신은요?
에밀리: 치즈 케이크 한 조각에다 코카콜라 한 병을 마실려고 해요.
한나: 마음을 바꿨어요. 건강에 좋은 것을 먹으려고 해요. 그래서 대신 과일 한 조각을 먹겠어요.
에밀리: 좋은 생각이군요. 내 역시 건강에 좋은 것을 먹겠어요. 녹차 한 컵을 마시겠어요.
한나: 우리가 먹는 것에 대해 보다 유의해야 겠어요.

02 Counting Uncountable Nouns.

Use count words when talking about uncountable nouns. Check the examples below.

a piece of cake	a plate of nachos
a can of beer	a slice of pizza
a bottle of juice	a bag of kimchi
a carton of milk	a loaf of bread
a box of cereal	a package of noodles

03 Write count words for the following uncountable nouns.

1. a ____________ of meat
2. a ____________ of rice
3. a ____________ of glasses
4. a ____________ of pie
5. a ____________ of chopsticks
6. a ____________ of sugar
7. a ____________ of grapes
8. a ____________ of fish
9. a ____________ of ice
10. a ____________ of lettuce
11. a ____________ of coffee
12. a ____________ of pickles
13. a ____________ of toothpaste
14. a ____________ of eggs
15. a ____________ of water

04 More Count Words.

Try to complete the count expressions with your partner.

1. a barrel of ________________
2. a tub of ________________
3. a bucket of ________________
4. a packet of ________________
5. a pint of ________________
6. a kilo of ________________
7. a ball of ________________
8. a bar of ________________
9. a pinch of ________________
10. a keg of ________________
11. a school of ________________
12. a swarm of ________________
13. a bouquet of ________________
14. a flock of ________________
15. a pot of ________________

05 Make sentences using some of the count expressions.

Ex) A school of fish swam under the boat.

1. (a barrel of) ____
2. (a bucket of) ____
3. (a pinch of) ____
4. (a swarm of) ____
5. (a flock of) ____
6. (a bouquet of) ____
7. (a pot of) ____
8. (a tub of) ____

Section 04 Conversation 3

01 Listen to the conversation and practice it with your partner.

Michael: How much studying did you do for the exam?

Taylor: I studied a lot. I always make sure I'm ready. What about you?

Michael: I didn't study a whole lot. I've had a ton of reading in my other courses to catch up on.

Taylor: You look tired, too. Did you get much sleep last night?

Michael: I only got about 4 hours of sleep. But I think I'll be ok.

Taylor: The teacher said some of the questions will be easy so don't worry.

마이클: 시험 공부를 얼마나 많이 했나요?
테일러: 공부를 많이 했어요. 나는 언제나 준비되어 있어요. 당신은요?
마이클: 나는 공부를 많이 하지 못했어요. 다른 과목에서 밀린 읽을 거리가 산더미처럼 너무 많았어요.
테일러: 당신도 피곤해 보여요. 지난 밤에 잠을 많이 잤어요?
마이클: 단지 4시간 정도 잤어요. 그러나 괜찮을 거라고 생각해요.
테일러: 선생님은 문제들 중 일부는 쉬울거라고 하시면서 걱정마라고 하셨어요.

02 Measuring Uncountable Words.

Uncountable nouns can also be measured in units like grams, kilos, pounds, tons, ounces and so forth. Check the examples below.

Ex) I have **a ton** of homework to do.

Ex) We need to lose **a few pounds**.

Ex) She bought **500 grams** of meat.

Ex) There is not **an ounce** of truth to that story.

Ex) We cooked **10 kilos** of rice.

03 Feelings.

Uncountable things like feelings such as happiness, love, anger, excitement and so forth can be measured by using words like **a little bit**, **some**, and **a lot**.

Ex) There was **a lot** of happiness in the room after the baby was born.

Ex) There were **some** angry people at the demonstration.

Ex) The dancers were **a little bit** excited before the show started.

Try using a little bit, some, and a lot to explain feelings.

1. (a little bit) ____

2. (some) ____

3. (a lot) ____

Section 05 Review

01 Make sentences using the following adverbs of frequency.

1. ______________________________ 3 times a day.
2. ______________________________ a lot.
3. ______________________________ every hour,
4. ______________________________ all the time.
5. ______________________________ only on Wednesday.
6. He almost never ______________________________.
7. I rarely ______________________________.
8. ______________________________ from time to time.
9. ______________________________ once in a while.

02 Answer the following questions with a partner.

1. How often do you eat out with your parents?
2. How often do you go to the beach?
3. How much do you like English class?
4. How much fun did you have on your last vacation?
5. How often do you go to the sauna?
6. How much stress do you get from studying English?
7. How much sleep did you get last night?
8. How often do you eat Chinese food?

UNIT

12 Suggestions

Section 01 Vocabulary

- □ bad temper: 성마른 기질
- □ bare facts: 있는 그대로의 사실
- □ bother you: 귀찮게 하다, 신경쓰이게 하다
- □ chain smoker: 줄 담배를 피우는 사람
- □ client: 클라이언트[고객]
- □ cover the cost: 비용을 충당하다
- □ details: 세부사항
- □ forest: 숲, 산림
- □ fresh air: 신선한 공기
- □ good chance: 좋은 기회
- □ handle things: 일을 처리하다
- □ interview: 면접, 인터뷰
- □ lonely: 외로운, 쓸쓸한
- □ peace and quiet: 평온, 고요함
- □ raining heavily: 비가 심하게 내리는
- □ secretly: 비밀히, 몰래
- □ slow down: 느긋해지다[속도 · 진행]을 늦추다
- □ special bonus: 특별보너스
- □ spend all day: 하루종일 보내다
- □ stick to: ~을 고수하다, ~을 계속하다
- □ stressed out: 스트레스로 지친, 스트레스가 쌓인
- □ tough time: 어려운 시기
- □ quit smoking: 금연
- □ wilderness: 황야, 황무지

Section 02 Conversation 1

01 Listen to the conversation and practice it with your partner.

Min Su: I'm so stressed out these days. I need to take a vacation.

Chris: What's bothering you?

Min Su: I need to get away from the city, the crowds of people, and the noise. I can't take it anymore. Everyone is making me crazy.

Chris: If you want to get away from all that, you should go to Canada. Go camping in the forest, go fishing in the wilderness. There is plenty of fresh air, peace, and quiet, and nobody to bother you.

Min Su: That's just what I need. I have a friend in Vancouver. I ought to give him a call and see if he would like to go camping for a couple of weeks.

Chris: All you need is your passport and a plane ticket. I can handle things here at work while you're gone.

민수: 나는 요즘 꽤 스트레스를 받고 있어요. 휴가가 필요해요.

크리스: 무엇이 당신을 괴롭히고 있나요?

민수: 도시, 군중 그리고 소음으로부터 벗어나는 것이 필요해요. 더이상 견딜 수 없어요. 모든 사람들이 나를 짜증나게 해요.

크리스: 당신이 모든 것으로부터 벗어나고 싶다면, 캐나다로 가세요. 숲에서 캠핑을 하고 야생에서 낚시를 하세요. 신선한 공기, 평화, 그리고 고요함이 넉넉히 있어요. 그 누구도 당신을 귀찮게 하지 않아요.

민수: 그것은 바로 내가 필요로 한 것이에요. 벤쿠버에 친구가 있어요. 그에게 전화를 해서 만약 그가 2주 정도 캠핑을 가고 싶어하는지 알아봐야겠어요.

크리스: 당신이 필요한 것은 여권과 비행기표이고요. 당신이 없는 동안 여기 일들은 내가 처리할게요.

02 Modal Verbs.

Should + Verb	Ought to + Verb

The expressions **should** and **ought to** can be used to make suggestions. These are only suggestions and are not necessary or required. **Should** is more commonly used than **ought to**.

Ex) He **should** quit smoking.

Ex) She **ought to** exercise more.

Need to + Verb	Must + Verb

The expressions **need to** and **must** are used mostly to talk about things that are very strongly suggested or required.

Ex) We **need to** be there at 9:00AM.

Ex) The report **must** be done by 6:00PM today.

>> Complete the sentences using should, ought to, need to or must.

1. We ______________ eat something before we go.
2. You ______________ put out the campfire before you leave.
3. You ______________ call your mother on her birthday.
4. Where ____________ we go after school?
5. People ____________ to eat and drink every day
6. People ____________ eat healthy food.
7. He ______________ pay the taxi driver before getting out of the cab.
8. She ______________ talk to her boyfriend if she's lonely.

9. Students ___________ not skip the final exam.

10. If it is raining heavily you ___________ use an umbrella.

03 Talking About Needs.

Make a team of 3 students and ask each other the following questions.

What do you need	Student 1	Student 2	Student 3
to do every day?			
to do tonight?			
to do tomorrow?			
to do this weekend?			

Give advice for each of the situations listed below. Use should or shouldn't.

1. Jung Hoon is overweight. ______________________________

2. Austin is a chain smoker. ______________________________

3. Martin is losing his hair. ______________________________

4. Min Su has a lot of stress. ______________________________

5. Jessica talks too much. ______________________________

6. Tyler wants to marry his girlfriend. ______________________________

7. Ashley is a terrible cook. ______________________________

8. Hannah won the lottery. ______________________________

9. Sarah is very lonely. ______________________________

10. Jacob has a bad temper. ______________________________

Section 03 Conversation 2

01 Listen to the conversation and practice it with your partner.

Nick: I need to start making some money, but I'm having a tough time finding a job.

Samantha: You should show me your resume. Maybe I can help you with it. How long is it?

Nick: My resume is four pages long. I wrote everything I could think of.

Samantha: You really need to keep a resume to one page. A four page resume is just too long.

Nick: So do you think I should just stick to the bare facts?

Samantha: That's right. You should talk about the details in the cover letter or at the job interview.

닉: 돈을 좀 벌기 시작할 필요가 있어요. 그러나 일자리를 구하는데 어려운 시기를 겪고 있어요.
사만타: 이력서를 보여 주세요. 당신을 도와드릴 수 있을 것 같군요. 길이는 얼마나 되나요?
닉: 내 이력서는 4페이지이구요. 내가 생각할 수 있는 모든 걸 적었어요.
사만타: 이력서가 1페이지로 되게 할 필요가 있어요. 4페이지 이력서는 너무 길어요.
닉: 그래서 단지 있는 그대로의 사실만을 고수해야 한다고 생각하세요?
사만타: 그래요. 자세한 것에 대해서는 커버레터에서나 혹은 직무인터뷰에서 말하세요.

02 Exercise.

Answer the following questions.

1. What do you need to do after graduation? ______________________

2. What do you need to do before getting married? ______________________

3. What should you do for your father on his birthday? ______________________

4. How long must a Korean man stay in the army? ______________________

5. What should you do before going to bed? ______________________

03 Together with your partner, give advice for each of the following situations.

1. You sleep in and miss your final exam.

____

2. You forgot your mother's birthday.

____

3. Your best friend's boyfriend/girlfriend is secretly dating another person.

____

4. You arrive home and realize you lost your smart phone.

____

5. Your friends want to eat at an expensive restaurant but you don't have enough money.

____

6. Your brother/sister is failing school because they spend all day playing computer games.

____

7. Your friend is thinking about buying a new car.

____

8. Your friend is thinking about taking a trip to the U.S.

____

Section 04 Conversation 3

01 Listen to the following conversation and practice it with your partner.

Kayla: You ought to join the school water sports club with me.

Alexis: Why do you think we should join that club?

Kayla: Well, we both need to get in better shape so we can go swimming at the beach.

Alexis: Is there a membership fee for the sports club?

Kayla: We must pay 10,000 won per month to join, because they need that money to cover the cost of the sports equipment and use of the pool.

Alexis: Okay, sounds good. It'll also be a good chance to make some new friends.

카일라: 나와 함께 학교 수상스포츠클럽에 가입해야 해요.

알렉시스: 왜 그 클럽에 가입해야 한다고 생각하세요?

카일라: 저, 우리 두 사람 모두 바닷가에 수영을 가기 위해서는 좋은 몸을 유지하는 것이 필요해서요.

알렉시스: 그 스포츠클럽에 회비가 있나요?

카일라: 가입을 위해서는 매월 1만원을 지불해야 해요. 왜냐하면 스포츠 장비와 풀장이용에 따른 비용을 충당할 돈이 필요하기 때문이죠.

알렉시스: 예, 좋아요. 또한 새로운 친구들을 사귈 수 있는 좋은 기회도 되겠군요.

02 So, Because, & Since.

You can use the words **so**, **because**, and **since** to connect ideas or sentences. When using **so**, the first part of the sentence is a statement and the second part of the sentence is the result of the first statement.

Ex) That's too expensive, **so** I am not going to buy it.
Ex) I passed the job interview, **so** I am going to take you all out for dinner.
Ex) She broke up with her boyfriend, **so** she is single again.
Ex) It's really hot, **so** we are going to the beach.

When using **because** and **since**, the part of the sentence that begins with **because** or **since** gives the reason and the other part gives the result.

Ex) **Because** it is too expensive, I won't buy it.
Ex) **Since** I passed the job interview, I am going to take you all out for dinner.
Ex) She is single again **because** she broke up with her boyfriend.
Ex) We are going to the beach **since** it's really hot.

>> Complete the following sentences using because, so or since.

1. Hannah wants to be a doctor, ____.

2. Fred is not popular ____.

3. ______________________________, Emily has been really happy.

4. ______________________________, we received a special bonus from the company.

5. They enjoyed the trip ____.

>> Answer the following questions using because, so or since.

1. Why do you go to school?

____

2. Why do so many people like computer games?

____

3. How long has it been since you downloaded a movie?

____

4. How long has it been since you called your parents?

____

5. Why do students like to have a party after final exams?

____

03 Put it Together.

Try to make suggestions using **ought to**, **should**, **must** and **need to** in a sentence together with **because**, **so** or **since**. Check the examples below and try to make sentences of your own.

Ex) You **must** stop at the red light, **so** you should slow down.
Ex) **Since** it's her birthday, you **should** buy her flowers.
Ex) She **ought to** get up early **because** she doesn't want to be late for the job interview.
Ex) He **must** be there on time **because** the client will arrive at 2:00 PM.

1. (should, because) ______________________________

2. (need to, since) ______________________________

3. (must, so) ______________________________

4. (ought to, because) ______________________________

5. (should, since) ______________________________

6. (need to, so) ______________________________

7. (must, because) ______________________________

8. (should, so) ______________________________

9. (need to, because) ______________________________

10. (must, since) ______________________________

11. (should, since) ______________________________

12. (should, because) ______________________________

UNIT

13

Travel & Transportation

Section 01 Vocabulary

Section 02 Conversation 1

Section 03 Travel

Section 04 Your Dream Vacation

Section 05 Conversation 3

Section 01 Vocabulary

□ advantages: 유리한 점, 이점

□ aisle seat: 통로 쪽 좌석

□ appropriate: 적절한

□ boarding: 탑승

□ commute: 통근하다, 통근

□ customer service desk: 고객서비스 데스크

□ dangerous: 위험한

□ definitely: 분명히, 확실히

□ departure: 출발

□ expecting: 예상[기대]하는

□ emergency exit: 비상구

□ gate number: 탑승구[출입구] 번호

□ imagine: 상상하다, 그리다

□ kill some time: 얼마동안 시간을 좀 때우다

□ laser light show: 레이저 광선쇼

□ my pleasure: 저도 기뻐요 (고맙다는 말에 대한 정중한 인사)

□ night market: 야시장

□ polite question: 예의바른[공손한, 정중한] 질문

□ restroom: 화장실

□ shuttle bus: 셔틀버스

□ window seat: 창가쪽 좌석

Section 02 Conversation 1 - Transportation

01 Listen to the following conversation and practice it with your partner.

Matthew: How long is your commute into school each day?

Kayla: It takes me about one hour to get to school. I take a shuttle bus to the subway station and then take the subway to the school.

Matthew: I take the bus. If the traffic is okay I can get to school in about 20 minutes. So, what do you do while traveling on the subway?

Kayla: I usually read or study. It's a great way to kill some time and get some work done, too.

Matthew: That's a really smart way to use your time. I usually play games on my smart phone when I take the bus.

Kayla: I like to play games, too, but only after my school work is done.

매튜: 매일 학교로 출퇴근 시간이 얼마나 걸리는지요?

카일라: 학교에 도착하는데 약 1시간 정도 걸려요. 셔틀버스를 타고 지하철역으로 가서 그리고 지하철을 타고 학교에 가요.

매튜: 나는 버스를 타요. 교통이 좋으면 약 20분 안에 학교에 도착할 수 있어요. 그런데, 지하철로 이동하는 동안 무엇을 하세요?

카일라: 나는 보통 독서하거나 공부를 해요. 그것은 시간을 보내고 어떤 일을 처리하는데도 좋은 방법이죠.

매튜: 그것 정말로 시간을 이용하는데 현명한 방법이군요. 나는 보통 버스를 탈 때 나의 스마트폰 상에서 게임을 해요.

카일라: 나 역시 게임하기를 좋아해요. 그러나 방과 후에만 게임을 해요.

02 Ask and answer the following questions together with your partner.

1. How do you get to school/work each day? ______________________

2. How long does it take you to get there? ______________________

3. How do you kill your time on the bus or subway? ______________________

4. Do you have a driver's license? ______________________

5. What are the advantages of having a car? ______________________

6. What kind of transportation do you prefer? ______________________

7. What is the most dangerous kind of transportation? ______________________

8. If you could buy any car, what would you buy? ______________________

03 Ask and answer the following questions together with your partner.

Make a team of 3 people and ask each other the following questions.

When you take a long trip in a car	Student 1	Student 2	Student 3
what do you do to kill the time?			
do you stop often along the way?			
what do you usually eat?			

Section 03 Travel

01 Answer the following travel questions.

1. Do you like to travel?

____

2. Who do you like to travel with?

____

3. Where do you usually sleep when you travel?

____

4. What do you like to take with you when you travel?

____

5. Have you been to Jeju Island?

____

6. Where is your favorite place to visit in Korea?

____

7. What other countries have you been to?

____

8. What place would you definitely not travel to?

____

9. What do you like to do when you travel?

____

10. What do you like to buy when you travel?

____

02 Traveling.

Ask and answer the following questions with your partner.

1. What is your favorite way to travel? ______________________________
2. Why do you like to travel that way the most? ______________________________
3. Where have you traveled to by airplane? ______________________________
4. In an airplane would you prefer the aisle or window seat? ______________________________
5. What do you think is the scariest way to travel? ______________________________

03 Airplane Vocabulary.

Below are some common vocabulary words for airplane travel.

□ airport tax : 공항세	□ departure : 출발
□ baggage claim : 수하물 찾는 곳	□ flight number : 항공편[비행기]번호
□ carry-on-bag : (가내)휴대용 가방	□ final boarding call : 마지막 탑승안내 방송
□ check in : 탑승수속	□ general boarding call : 일반 탑승안내 방송
□ reservation : 예약	□ lavatory : 화장실
□ checked baggage : 위탁수하물	□ pre-boarding call : 정각이전 탑승안내 방송
□ connecting flight : 연결항공편	□ security : 안전, 보안

04 Conversation 2.

Listen to the conversation and practice it with your partner.

Min Su: Has the plane started boarding yet? I see some people going in.

Keun: They just made the pre-boarding call. Those people boarding now are elderly, disabled, and parents with small children. They will make the general boarding call soon.

Min Su: Did you get a window or aisle seat?

Keun: I got an aisle seat. I don't want to bother anyone if I get up and move around.

Min Su: I am sitting at the emergency exit. I like that spot because there is more leg room.

Keun: Don't forget to read the safety card in the seat pocket. The flight attendant will be expecting you to help her if there is an emergency.

민수: 비행기 탑승이 벌써 시작되었나요? 몇몇 사람들이 들어가고 있어요.

근: 방금 정각이전 탑승방송을 했어요. 지금 탑승하는 사람들은 노인, 장애인, 어린아이들을 동반한 부모입니다. 곧 일반 탑승안내 방송이 나오겠군요.

민수: 당신은 창가좌석 또는 통로쪽 좌석을 구했나요?

근: 통로쪽 좌석을 구했어요. 내가 일어나서 이동할 때 누구에게 신경쓰게 하고 싶지 않아요.

민수: 나는 비상구에 앉아 있어요. 다리를 뻗을 공간이 넓어서 그 자리를 좋아해요.

근: 좌석 앞 주머니에 있는 안전카드를 꼭 읽어보세요. 승무원은 위급한 상황이 발생할 경우 당신이 도와주기를 기대할 것이니까요.

05 Make sentences or questions using the following vocabulary.

Ex) How much is the **airport tax**?

Ex) The **baggage claim** area was very crowded.

1. (carry-on-bag) ______________________________

2. (check in) ______________________________

3. (checked baggage) ______________________________

4. (connecting flight) ______________________________

5. (departure) ______________________________

6. (flight number) ______________________________

7. (pre-boarding call) ______________________________

8. (general boarding call) ______________________________

9. (final boarding call) ______________________________

10. (lavatory) ______________________________

11. (reservation) ______________________________

12. (security) ______________________________

Section 04 Your Dream Vacation

01 Plan a dream vacation with a group of students.

Make a team of 3 people. Imagine you and your friends are taking a trip around the world. You can stop in 5 countries. What countries would you like to visit? How long would you stay? What would you do there?

Ex) We would go to Hawaii first. / We will stay for 1 week. / We would see the volcano.

Where would you go?	How long would you stay?	What would you do there?
1. ________	1. ________	1. ________
2. ________	2. ________	2. ________
3. ________	3. ________	3. ________
4. ________	4. ________	4. ________
5. ________	5. ________	5. ________

02 Activity.

Look at the three ads for tours and then answer the questions below.

Hong Kong City Tour	**Harbor Tour**	**Temple Tour**
See the sights of the city. Visit Victoria Peak, go shopping at the night market.	See the sights of Hong Kong from the water. Visit Discovery Bay, see the night time laser light show.	Visit Wong Tai Sin Temple. See traditional Chinese architecture and culture.
Cost: $30 USD	Cost: $25 USD	Cost: $35 USD
Tel: 010 545 8282	Tel: 010 545 1818	Tel: 010 545 6767

1. Which tour is the most expensive? ______________________________

2. Which tour is the cheapest? ______________________________

3. Which tour goes to Victoria Peak? ______________________________

4. Which tour is not at night? ______________________________

5. Which tour would you like to take? ______________________________

Section 05 Conversation 3 – Being Polite

01 Listen to the following conversation and practice it with your partner.

Sun Hee: Excuse me, sir. Could you tell me how I can get to the convention center from here?

Tyler: Sure, you can get on bus number 17. It stops at the corner over there.

Sun Hee: Is it far away from here?

Tyler: No, ma'am, it's about a 10 minute drive. You could even take a taxi there.

Sun Hee: Thank you so much.

Tyler: No problem. My pleasure.

선희: 실례합니다, 여기에서 컨벤션 센터에 어떻게 가는지 가르쳐 주시겠어요?
타일러: 그럴게요. 17번 버스편이 있어요. 저기 코너에서 정차해요.
선희: 여기서 먼가요?
타일러: 아니오, 부인. 차로 10분 정도 걸려요. 거기에는 택시를 탈 수도 있어요.
선희: 대단히 고마워요.
타일러: 무슨 말씀을요. 저도 기뻐요.

02 Can You, Could You, Please, Excuse Me, Pardon Me & Thank You.

When starting a conversation with a person you do not know it is best to start with the expression **excuse me** or **pardon me**. The expressions **could you** and **can you** are used to ask for something. **Can** is more informal than **could** and is best used with people you know well. **Could** is more appropriate for people you don't know well. Also using the word **please** at the end of your question makes it more polite. Also remember to say **thank you** to the person for helping you.

Ex) Excuse me, sir. Could you tell me where the bus stop is located, please?

Ex) Pardon me, miss. Could you tell me the departure time, please?

03 Imagine you are traveling overseas and asking questions to people you don't know. Write a polite question for each situation.

1. You want to know the gate number for your flight.

____

2. You want to know the way to the Korean restaurant.

____

3. You would like a worker to call a taxi for you.

____

4. You would like to know when the hotel shuttle bus arrives.

____

5. You would like to know when the night market opens.

____

6. You would like to know where the restroom is.

____

7. You would like to know where the customer service desk is located.

____

8. You would like to know when the last train leaves for the airport.

____

UNIT

14

Health

Section 01 Vocabulary

Section 02 Conversation 1

Section 03 Conversation 2

Section 04 Conversation 3

Section 01 Vocabulary

- □ allergies: 과민한 신체적 반응현상
- □ avoid: 피하다, 회피하다
- □ bad reaction: 나쁜 반응
- □ chest cold: 기침 감기
- □ cough: 기침, 기침하다
- □ emergency room: 응급실
- □ emergency situation: 응급상황
- □ fluids: 유체, 유동체
- □ head cold: 코감기
- □ itchy: 가려운
- □ medical care: 의료, 건강관리
- □ medical emergency: 응급의료
- □ medical history: 병력
- □ medication: 약물치료, 투약
- □ overnight: 밤사이에, 하룻밤 동안
- □ plenty: 풍부[충분]한 양(의~), 풍부한
- □ prescribe: 처방을 내리다, 처방하다
- □ rash: 발진, 뾰루지
- □ really hurts: 정말로 아프다
- □ sprained: [발목 · 손목 따위를] 삔
- □ surgery: 외과, 수술
- □ traditional medicine: 전통의료
- □ twisted ankle: 접질린 발목
- □ wisdom tooth: 사랑니

Section 02 Conversation 1 - Feeling Sick

01 Listen to the following conversation and practice it with your partner.

Sarah: Oh my goodness Min Su, that cough sounds terrible.

Min Su: I think I better get it checked out by the doctor.

Sarah: There is a really bad chest cold going around these days.

Min Su: I've had this cough since I met my brother. And he had a bad chest cold. So I think I caught it from him.

Sarah: Anyway you should go see a doctor, get some medicine, and take a rest.

Min Su: You're right. I've had this cough for 3 days and it is not getting any better. I'll go see the doctor after lunch.

사라: 어머나, 민수씨, 기침이 심하군요.

민수: 의사의 진찰을 받아보려고 해요.

사라: 요즘 유행하고 있는 아주 심한 기침 감기가 있어요.

민수: 내 동생을 만난 이래로 계속되고 있어요. 그는 심한 기침 감기에 걸렸었는데 그를 통해서 기침감기가 걸렸다고 생각해요.

사라: 어쨌든 의사에게 가 보는 게 좋겠어요. 약도 좀 사고 그리고 휴식을 취하세요.

민수: 당신 말이 맞아요. 3일 동안 계속 기침을 해왔는데 차도가 없어요. 점심 식사 후 병원에 가 볼려고 해요.

02 Body Parts.

Practice your pronunciation of the following body parts. Then put the correct body part word in the picture.

1. eye	눈	2. neck	목	3. wrist	손목
4. lower back	허리	5. nose	코	6. elbow	팔꿈치
7. shoulder	어깨	8. chin	볼	9. knee	무릎
10. thumb	엄지손가락	11. chest	가슴	12. stomach	위
13. hand	손	14. toe	발가락	15. mouth	입
16. ear	귀	17. throat	목구멍	18. finger	손가락
19. upper leg	대퇴	20 lower leg	하퇴	21. upper arm	상박
22. lower arm	하박	23. head	머리	24. ankle	발목

Human Body Parts

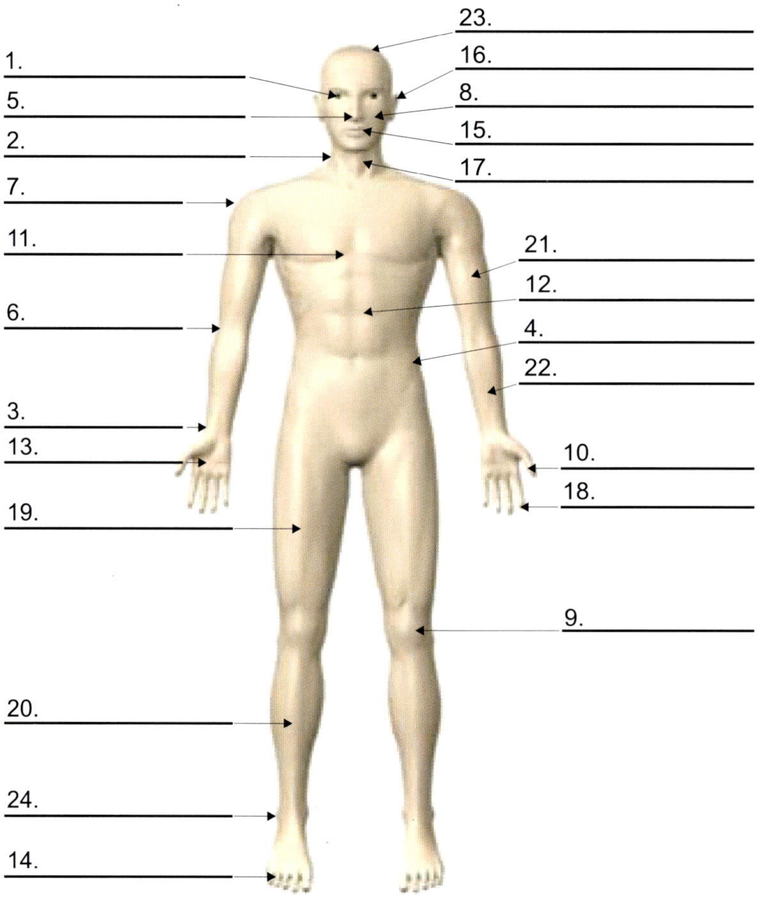

03 Using A, An, The.

Conversation Point!

The words **a**, **an**, and **the** are called articles. They behave like adjectives by modifying nouns. **The** is a **definite** article and clearly identifies what it refers to. Example: the dog, the test, the teacher, the score. **A** and **an** are called **indefinite** articles. For example the expression "Call a policeman." means call ***any*** policeman not a specific police officer. **An** works in the same way. For example "An animal in the forest made a noise." means ***any*** animal without specifying what exact animal made the noise.

Practice putting **a**, **the**, or **an** in the correct blank.

1. Jung Hoon spent _____ week in _____ city hospital.

2. Ashley is going to see _______ doctor after work today.

3. _______ apple a day keeps the doctor away.

4. The nurse said to take _______ medicine and get some sleep.

5. The ambulance arrived and took the old man to _________ hospital.

6. The soccer player twisted his ankle and can't play in ________ next game.

7. She is going to have ________ surgery tomorrow and will stay in the hospital for 3 days.

8. She had _______ baby boy and I am going to _________ hospital to see them.

9. _________ emergency room at _________ children's hospital is quite busy.

10. There is ________ emergency situation at the ice rink.

04 Talking about Pain.

When you talk about pain there are different expressions you can use to explain it. The most common expressions are **pain**, **ache**, **hurt**, and **sore**. Check the examples below.

Ex) I have a **pain** in my stomach.
Ex) He has a lot of **pain** in the lower back.
Ex) I have a **pain** in my chest.

Ex) I have a tooth**ache**.
Ex) I have an ear**ache**.
Ex) I have a head**ache**.

Ex) I have a **sore** throat.
Ex) I have a **sore** knee.
Ex) I have a **sore** foot.

Ex) My arm **hurts**.
Ex) The shoulder **hurts** a lot.
Ex) My back **hurts**.

05 Expressing Yourself.

Make sentences using the vocabulary words below with the expressions **pain**, **ache**, **sore**, or **hurt**.

1. (finger) ______________________________
2. (elbow) ______________________________
3. (head) ______________________________
4. (wrist) ______________________________
5. (tooth) ______________________________
6. (ankle) ______________________________
7. (back) ______________________________
8. (shoulder) ______________________________
9. (neck) ______________________________
10. (knee) ______________________________

Section 03 Conversation 2

01 Listen to the conversation and practice it with your partner.

Michael: Doctor Lee, I feel terrible. My muscles ache and my head really hurts.

Doctor: Let me check your temperature. Hmm…you've got a fever. How long have you been feeling like this?

Michael: For about two days now. What do you think is the matter?

Doctor: It looks like you've got the flu. I am going to prescribe some medication for you. I want you to go home and stay in bed, get some rest and drink plenty of fluids.

Michael: Thank you, Doctor Lee.

Doctor: If you feel worse or have a bad reaction to the medication, come back in and see me.

마이클: 이 박사님, 정말 기분이 좋지 않군요. 근육통과 머리가 너무 아파요.

의사: 어디 체온을 재어 봅시다. 흠… 열이 있군요. 이러신지 얼마나 되셨죠?

마이클: 현재 2주 정도 됩니다. 문제가 무엇이라고 생각하세요?

의사: 독감에 걸린 듯 하군요. 약을 처방해 드릴께요. 댁으로 가셔서 침대에 머무르시면서 좀 쉬세요. 그리고 물을 많이 마시세요.

마이클: 고마워요, 이 박사님.

의사: 만약 더 안좋은 느낌이 있거나 약에 대해 나쁜 반응이 있으시면, 제게 오세요.

02 More Vocabulary.

When talking about an illness or health problem you may not know what the problem is. When talking to a doctor or nurse you can explain the problem by talking about the symptoms. Practice your pronunciation of the symptoms listed below.

I have ___________________________

a cough	a runny nose
nausea	stomach pain
a sore throat	a rash on my _______
swelling in my ______	a headache
a fever	a burn on my _______
a sharp pain in my _________	a toothache
chills	been vomiting

03 Match the explanations with the symptoms listed below.

1. Emily has stomach pain.	A. She has a fever.
2. Sarah's throat hurts.	B. He has a sprained ankle.
3. Ashley has a high temperature.	C. He has a sore back.
4. Min Su has a runny nose.	D. He has a headache.
5. Michael's head hurts a lot.	E. He has a rash.
6. Jacob cannot stand on his foot.	F. She has a sore throat.
7. Brandon has a sharp pain in his ear.	G. She has a toothache.
8. Chris cannot lift heavy things.	H. He has a head cold.
9. Samantha's wisdom tooth hurts.	I. He has an earache.
10. Nick has a red itchy spot on his skin.	J. She has a stomachache.

Section 04 Conversation 3

01 Listen to the conversation and practice it with your partner.

Man: 911 emergency. How can I help you?

Hannah: My friend just fell on the ice and hit her head.

Man: What is your location, miss?

Hannah: We're at the Central City Ice Rink.

Man: Stay with your friend. An ambulance is on route and will be there shortly.

Hannah: Okay, but please hurry!

남자: 911응급대, 뭘 도와드릴까요?
한나: 내 친구가 방금 얼음 위에 넘어졌는데 머리를 부딪쳤어요.
남자: 지금 계신 곳이 어디시죠?
한나: 센트럴시티 아이스링크에 있어요.
남자: 친구와 함께 계세요. 구급차가 가고 있으니 거기에 곧 도착할 겁니다.
한나: 좋아요. 하지만 서둘러 주세요.

02 Emergency Situations.

Conversation Point!

Knowing your location and address is extremely important in a medical emergency. Knowing where you are helps emergency workers get to you as quickly as possible. Also different countries have different numbers for emergency situations. South Korea uses the number 119 while countries like the U.S. use 911. Make sure you know what number to call.

>> Exercise

Fill in the blanks with the correct vocabulary word.

moment	exactly	medications	anything	
keep	allergies	history	ambulance	area

1. The operator said the__________________ is on its way.
2. Please stay in the waiting __________________.
3. The doctor will be here in a ____________________.
4. Please try to ____________ still, sir.
5. We need you to tell us __________________ what happened.
6. Does she have any _____________ to medication?
7. Does he have a _____________ of problems like this?
8. Are you taking any ________________________?
9. Is there _______________ else we should know?

03 Health Talk.

Answer the following questions together with your partner.

1. Did you ever stay overnight in the hospital? What was the problem?

2. Have you ever been in an ambulance? If so, why?

3. What is the most important skill a nurse should have?

4. What do you think is the most difficult thing about being a doctor?

5. What kind of traditional medicine do you think works really well?

6. Do you think medical care should be free for all Koreans?

7. When you were a child what medicine did you hate taking?

8. What is the most important thing you can do to avoid getting sick?

Profile for Authors

■ Trevor B. Mitchell

Trevor B. Mitchell has a Master of Adult Education and a B.A. from St. Francis Xavier University in Antigonish, Nova Scotia, Canada. He also holds a Bachelor of University Studies in education from the University of Maine at Fort Kent, USA. Trevor has taught English in Korea since 1997. He has worked as a business English professor at Ewha Women's University from 2000-2006, and since then continues to teach English for the Department of Management at Dongyang Mirae University in Seoul. His research interests include curriculum and program evaluation.

■ Stephen L. Poirier

Stephen Poirier is from Canada and currently resides in Seoul, Korea. He has an MA in History from the University of Western Ontario and a Certificate of Technical Writing from Carleton University. Stephen has worked for over 20 years as an English language instructor in Korea, Russia, and Canada, and for two years as a history professor in Canada.

■ Baek Ju Hyun

Baek Ju Hyun received his Ph.D. in management from Korea University in Seoul, Korea. He received a special certificate for the Management and Business English program from San Diego State University, USA. He currently teaches Economics, International Business and Business English at Dongyang Mirae University in Seoul, Korea. His research interests include International Economics and Business.

Everyday English

2014년 9월 1일 1판 1쇄 발행
2020년 3월 5일 2판 1쇄 인쇄
2020년 3월 10일 2판 1쇄 발행

저 자 Trevor B. Mitchell
Stephen L. Poirier
Baek Ju Hyun

발행인 류재식 · 박용범
발행처 도서출판 북넷

서울시 용산구 효창원로 70길 46 대신빌딩 2층
등 록 2010년 6월 7일(제2010-000069호)
전 화 (02) 395-2341
팩 스 (02) 395-2303

정가 25,000원

ISBN 978-89-98581-20-6

e-mail : book2341@naver.com